AI TO A+

MASTERING THE ART OF AI CONTENT CRAFTING

SHANU SHAH

HAY HOUSE

HAY HOUSE INDIA
New Delhi • London • Sydney
Carlsbad, California • New York City

Hay House Publishers (India) Pvt Ltd
Muskaan Complex, Plot No. 3, B-2, Vasant Kunj, New Delhi – 110070, India

Hay House LLC, P.O. Box 5100, Carlsbad, CA 92018-5100, USA
Hay House UK Ltd, 1st Floor, Crawford Corner, 91-93 Baker Street, London W1U 6QQ, UK
Hay House Australia Publishing Pty Ltd, 18/36 Ralph St., Alexandria NSW 2015, Australia

Email: contact@hayhouse.co.in
Website: www.hayhouse.co.in

First published by Hay House India, 2025
Reprint, 2025
11 10 9 8 7 6 5 4 3 2

ISBN 978-93-66112-54-1
ISBN 978-93-66119-02-1 (E-Book)

Printed at Repro India Ltd

FSC www.fsc.org MIX Paper from responsible sources FSC® C047271

Hay House is committed to a sustainable future for our business, our readers and our planet. This book is made from Forest Stewardship Council® certified paper.

To Dhaval,
for bringing more love and joy into my life than
I ever could have imagined.

Contents

Part III: Customisation

Prologue

I have been a writer since my earliest memories, crafting heartbreak-themed poems even before experiencing the nuances of romantic love. Apparently, one doesn't need a romantic relationship to encounter heartbreak; families offer plenty of material. My initiation into the literary world occurred in 2019 with my first novel, *The Victim*, an exhilarating high-paced action thriller. I was confident that I would secure the prestigious writers' award, but I found myself without it. This prompted introspection, leading me to question the quality of my narrative and the adequacy of my writing style.

To refine my skills, I immersed myself in extensive research, studying not only bestselling works but also the lives of eminent authors. Their online presence, personal experiences, and the motivations behind their literary creations became focal points of my investigation. My desk now holds a wealth of information awaiting organisation, synthesis, and eventual publication.

Alongside my literary pursuits, 2020 marked a professional milestone as I assumed the role of Centre

Head, ushering in increased responsibilities at work. Although my workload escalated, the perks of overseeing a growing team allowed for pockets of free time. While designing training calendars for IELTS and other English language courses and formulating digital marketing strategies, I continued to write. Not long after, I crafted a blog that featured horror stories. However, I found myself lacking satisfaction, perhaps something was still anomalous. Upon reflection, I discovered that my level of focus and dedication differed significantly when producing academic essays, YouTube scripts, captions, and internal circulation materials for companies—specifically those related to grammar, essay writing, and various other topics. The realisation that I may be better suited for non-fiction writing brought both joy and uncertainty.

I then started my research on a book called *How to Make Your Essays Band 9 Worthy.* I thought the students would love the book. However, my foray into crafting helpful band 9 essays for IELTS students revealed a disheartening truth. Many students, fixated on securing the minimum score for admission and visa purposes, dismissed the pursuit of excellence as an unnecessary endeavour. One of my committed students, displaying considerable potential, exerted effort sufficient to achieve a score of 6.5 bands in the IELTS exams. To my astonishment, he successfully attained a score of 6.5 bands in the final IELTS exam, securing admission and obtaining a visa concurrently. While his approach was successful, my method for writing *How to Write a Band 9 Worthy Essay* ended up staying in my Google Drive.

It is crucial to remember that failures consistently offer valuable lessons. In my case, the lesson was about understanding reader behaviour. When it comes to the purchasing habits of non-fiction readers, it is evident that they aren't merely buying a book; they are seeking a solution to a problem. They prefer to avoid unnecessary details, get straight to the point, and evaluate the effectiveness of the proposed solution. Moreover, my professional journey also provided deep insights into consumer behaviour, which guided the direction of the books I wanted to write. With this newfound perspective, I embarked on a new path, starting a blog and researching the intricacies of effective writing.

The culmination of my efforts materialised in the form of the manuscript, *How to Write a Self-Help Book,* stemming from research initiated in 2020. While some insights from this research are published on my blog, *The Skillful Minds,* the manuscript itself remained half-finished. Eventually, the manuscript was scooted aside, when I learnt about ChatGPT. I soon discovered that a single line, crafted with the right prompt, could produce significant content, demonstrating an efficiency that was unmatched by any of my past writing experiences.

As time progressed, ChatGPT's predictive tendencies led to a decline in the quality of online content. Phrases like 'realm of', 'delve into', and 'unleash the power of', 'in the grand tapestry of' became unmistakable indicators of ChatGPT's influence. This realisation sparked a eureka moment, leading me to shift my research focus and begin working on this book. In the midst of this, Donabel from the Philippines extended an invitation to train the generative AI models. I accepted the offer, but my attention swiftly shifted back to research and writing. While my collaboration with Donabel was brief, it provided valuable insights and intelligence that significantly enriched the content of this book. That short assignment also helped me design more comprehensive rubrics.

Through my professional journey, I realised that writing is not just about putting words on a page, but about understanding the needs and expectations of readers. This book is a culmination of that realisation. Within these pages, you will find 16 detailed rubrics designed to enhance the quality of AI-generated content, focusing on elements such as coherence, readability, tone appropriateness, and much more. By following these guidelines, you will learn how to craft content that not only meets but exceeds the expectations of your audience. Each chapter offers practical tips, real-world examples, and expert insights to help you master the nuances of AI content creation. Whether you are an experienced content developer or just beginning your journey, this book will serve as your comprehensive guide to becoming a skilled AI writer.

Introduction

As I step into the year 2024, I find myself in an era where algorithms give birth to words and machines shape the contours of ideas. The landscape of content creation is undergoing a rapid evolution, challenging the very essence of traditional writing norms. A Statista report revealed that ChatGPT alone boasts 17.48 million users worldwide, with a projected growth of 15 billion by 2030. Additionally, the generative artificial intelligence (AI) market is set for significant expansion, foreseeing a leap from $14 billion in 2020 to nearly $900 billion in 2023 and surpassing $1.3 trillion by 2032. This surge is fuelled by the proliferation of cutting-edge generative AI tools like Bard by Google, ChatGPT by OpenAI, and Midjourney by Midjourney Inc.

However, the job landscape for content writers presents an interesting contrast, with a mere 32,000 jobs available worldwide compared to the staggering 52,000 writers in the United States alone. This disparity suggests a growing inclination towards the use of generative AI for faster and cost-effective content creation. However, this trend has sparked a debate within the writing community: while some writers express disdain for generative AI users, others view it as a potential threat to creativity. Nevertheless, there has been a widespread adoption of AI for blogging, social media posts, and general online content creation.

Despite this surge, AI-generated content often exhibits a mechanical or AI-like quality, resulting in disengaged readers. Simply copying and pasting this content is not advisable, prompting the need for this book. Drawing from my experience as an IELTS trainer and freelance AI assistant writer—where I specialised in crafting and refining AI prompts based on specific rubrics—this book aims to guide you through the process of editing content generated by AI. The rubrics provided will help ensure that your content is engaging, compelling, and aligned with brand values, adding a more human touch. Additionally, the accompanying checklist will streamline your editing process.

As we dive deeper into the art of editing generative AI content, we will unravel intricacies, embrace challenges, and uncover strategies defining editorial excellence in an era dominated by technology. From mitigating biases to enhancing creativity, ensuring factual accuracy to preserving the human touch, this book serves as a guide to the nuanced art of refining content generated by tomorrow's machines.

Establishing the Essentials

Generative AI, short for generative artificial intelligence, refers to a category of artificial intelligence that involves machines creating or generating new content, data, or outputs. Unlike traditional AI systems that rely on pre-programmed rules and responses, generative AI has the ability to produce novel and contextually relevant outputs on its own.

One prominent example of generative AI is the use of neural networks, particularly generative models. These models are trained on extensive datasets and learn patterns, structures, and features, allowing them to create new content similar to their training data. Another well-known type of generative AI is the language model, which can produce human-like text based on the input it receives. OpenAI's GPT (Generative Pre-trained Transformer) models, such as GPT-4, are notable examples of generative AI that excel in tasks like natural language understanding and text generation.

Generative AI has applications in various fields, including natural language processing, image generation, and even music composition. While it holds great potential for creativity and problem-solving, ethical considerations, such as potential biases in generated content and plagiarism are crucial aspects to be mindful of in its development and deployment. In this chapter, we will explore all these aspects, delving into the technological innovations, creative possibilities, and ethical implications of generative AI, as well as discussing ways to navigate the challenges and harness their full potential responsibly.

Current Usage of Generative AI

In May 2023, WPP, the world's largest advertising agency announced a strategic partnership with chipmaker Nvidia to leverage generative AI for developing advertisements. The collaboration aims to empower WPP's creative teams by seamlessly integrating content from sources like Adobe and Getty Images into campaigns, enhancing efficiency and scalability.

In India, WPP collaborated with Mondelez for an AI-driven Cadbury campaign featuring Bollywood superstar Shah Rukh Khan during Diwali. The campaign utilised AI-generated versions of the actor in commercials, encouraging viewers to visit local stores. Simultaneously, French advertising giant Publicis Groupe revealed plans to acquire full ownership of Publicis Sapient AI Labs, an AI joint venture launched in 2020 with tech firms Elder Research and Tquila. This move reflects a broader trend, as a survey conducted in early 2023 found that one-fifth of US brand marketers aimed to enhance creative content development with their recent AI deployments. Additionally, seven out of ten marketers expressed excitement about

AI's potential for rapid market research on both prospective and existing customers. However, concerns about generative AI's implementation costs, legal vulnerabilities, and data privacy ranked as the top worries among US marketers. Projections suggest that by 2030, almost one-third of clerical positions in US ad agencies could be eliminated due to generative AI implementation. Furthermore, around one-fifth of sales-related jobs are also predicted to face workforce reductions.

This trend is underscored by a March 2023 survey in the United States, which found that 55 per cent of marketers are already utilising Chat GPT for their marketing needs. Additionally, 42 per cent of marketers have opted for Copy.ai, a natural language processing software known for generating product descriptions and social media content, to meet their marketing objectives. According to a Statista report, the monthly app downloads for Chap GPT have significantly peaked at 17.48 million from 4.16 in just 5 months.

Generative AI is rapidly transforming various industries, especially in the context of marketing and advertising, where it enables creative innovations and enhances efficiency. As companies continue to adopt this technology, its impact is becoming more pronounced, with significant changes in job roles and creative processes on the horizon. However, as generative AI becomes more integrated into these fields, it is essential for businesses to carefully consider its ethical implications, costs, and potential legal challenges. The landscape of generative AI is still evolving and staying informed and adaptable will be key for organisations looking to leverage its full potential responsibly and effectively.

How Generative AI Works?

In the vast landscape of technological marvels, generative artificial intelligence stands out as a fascinating fusion of human creativity and machine precision. At its core, generative AI is a subset of artificial intelligence that involves machines not just in recognising patterns or making decisions based on data but actually creating new content. This isn't the cold, calculated AI of the past; it is a new breed, capable of understanding context, generating human-like text, and even producing artistic creations. Let's look at how generative AI operates and employs sophisticated models to reshape the landscape of digital creation and offer unprecedented creative possibilities.

1. **Understanding the Foundation: Neural Networks**

   Neural networks consist of interconnected nodes, or artificial neurons, organised into layers. These layers work in harmony to process information. In the case of generative AI, the architecture often involves recurrent neural networks (RNNs) or transformers.

2. **Learning from Data: The Training Phase**

   To make AI truly generative, it needs to learn from data . . . lots of it. During the training phase, the AI model is fed vast amounts of diverse information, from articles and books to images and videos, depending on the application. This process allows the model to grasp the nuances of language, understand context, and discern patterns. This step is similar to exposing a child to a multitude of experiences to shape their understanding of the world.

3. **The Role of Parameters and Weights**

Within the neural network, parameters and weights play a crucial role. Parameters are the internal configurations that the model adjusts during training to fine-tune its understanding. On the other hand, weights determine the strength of connections between neurons. Through a complex optimisation process, the model refines these parameters and weights, gradually improving its ability to generate content.

4. **Generating New Content: The Magic Unfolds**

Once trained, a generative AI model becomes a creative tool. When given a prompt or context, it uses the patterns it has learnt to generate content. For text, this could range from coherent paragraphs to full articles. For images, it might involve creating realistic scenes or unique artworks. The model leverages its training to produce new and original content, often indistinguishable from what a human might create.

Diverse Applications of Generative AI

Generative AI is not confined to a single domain; its applications are vast and varied. It can assist writers in drafting articles, generate marketing copy, and even compose poetry. In design, it supports artists by suggesting visual elements or creating entirely new artworks. Chatbots powered by generative AI engage users in natural conversations, understanding context and delivering relevant responses.

Let's explore the most prominent applications and use cases of generative AI across different fields, examining how this technology is revolutionising industries and boosting creativity in both technical and artistic arenas.

1. **Content Creation**

   Generative AI, exemplified by models like OpenAI's GPT-3, is transforming content creation across sectors. Its remarkable capabilities in crafting human-like articles, marketing copy, and narratives signify a revolutionary shift. Businesses are leveraging generative AI to streamline processes, ensuring efficiency gains and prompt responses to evolving trends. Beyond efficiency, it collaborates with human creators, enhancing creativity and redefining the storytelling process. As we advance in understanding generative AI's impact, it becomes clear that this technology is a transformative force reshaping the landscape of content creation.

2. **Conversational Interfaces**

   Generative AI takes centre stage in crafting sophisticated conversational interfaces, powering chatbots and virtual assistants that engage users in natural and context-aware conversations. These interfaces redefine digital communication by simulating natural dialogues, thanks to advanced AI models that grasp context, tone, and user intent. Context-aware conversations distinguish generative AI interfaces, dynamically adapting responses for personalised and human-like interactions.

   In the domain of customer service, the user experience is substantially elevated as generative AI liberates users from rigid command structures, fostering intuitive, customised, and friendly interactions across platforms.

The adaptability of generative AI across diverse technological ecosystems positions it as a universal tool for communication enhancement. Notably, the technology's strength lies in providing instantaneous responses and solutions, meeting modern user expectations and contributing to business efficiency.

3. Creative Design

Generative AI is transforming the profession of creative design, presenting a revolutionary force that collaborates with human creativity to open new artistic possibilities. The application extends seamlessly to crafting logos, graphics, visual art, and much more, fostering a co-creative dynamic between designers and AI models.

Generative AI serves as a trusted collaborator, augmenting creative processes with fresh ideas and alternative perspectives, redefining traditional design methodologies. The symbiotic relationship between human intuition and AI-driven insights opens new avenues for artistic exploration, experimentation, and evolution.

4. Personalised Marketing

Generative AI is revolutionising marketing strategies by enabling the creation of customised content at scale. It leverages advanced algorithms to analyse user preferences, behaviours, and interactions, allowing marketers to craft customised messages that resonate with each consumer. This data-driven personalisation uncovers patterns in vast datasets, leading to emotionally resonant marketing that enhances customer engagement.

Generative AI also enables the creation of dynamic content based on real-time user interactions, moving beyond static advertisements. This personalised approach fosters stronger connections and loyalty among customers. Additionally, the scalability and efficiency of AI allow marketers to effectively reach diverse audiences, making campaigns more impactful and engaging.

5. Medical Research

Generative AI is at the forefront of reshaping healthcare, driving breakthroughs in medical research and drug discovery. The technology's remarkable capacity to swiftly analyse extensive datasets provides researchers with crucial insights, enabling them to identify potential drug candidates, predict patient responses, and assist in disease diagnosis. It also has a significant potential to expedite the development of life-saving medications, marking a new era of innovation and efficiency in the medical field and promising improved healthcare outcomes.

6. Code Generation

Generative AI is increasingly being employed for code generation and programming tasks. Developers can utilise AI models to generate code snippets, aiding in software development and reducing the time required for programming. This application enhances productivity and facilitates innovation in the software development lifecycle.

7. Simulation and Training

Generative AI helps create realistic simulations and training environments for various industries. From flight simulators for pilots to virtual training scenarios for healthcare professionals, AI-generated simulations offer immersive and effective training experiences, preparing individuals for real-world situations.

In summary, generative AI is completely changing the way we interact with technology, blurring the lines between human creativity and artificial intelligence. It is a step into a new paradigm where machines become not just tools but collaborators, augmenting our capabilities and expanding the horizons of what's possible.

How Generative AI Will Shape Content Creation and Digital Media

The future of generative AI has significant implications for content writing, blog creation, website development, and eBook production. It introduces a range of potential impacts that writers and content creators should consider, as outlined below:

1. **Efficiency and Speed:** Generative AI has the capability to automate the content creation process, significantly reducing the time required for writers to generate drafts, ideas, or complete articles.
2. **Content Ideation:** AI can be a valuable companion for writers in generating creative ideas. By analysing trends, user preferences, and relevant data, AI algorithms can suggest topics likely to resonate with the target audience.

3. **Personalisation:** Leveraging generative AI enables the creation of personalised content tailored to individual preferences, enhancing user engagement by delivering content aligned with readers' specific interests and needs.
4. **Quality Improvement:** AI can assist in proofreading, grammar checking, and ensuring overall content quality. This support helps writers produce polished and error-free content, contributing to an enhanced reading experience.
5. **Multilingual Content:** Generative AI's potential extends to facilitating the creation of content in multiple languages, breaking down language barriers, and expanding the reach of content to a global audience.
6. **Content Variations:** AI's ability to generate different content variations based on specific parameters proves beneficial for A/B testing scenarios or adapting content for different platforms and diverse audiences.
7. **AI-Enhanced Collaboration:** Writers can collaborate with AI tools to boost their creativity and refine their writing style. AI can provide suggestions, identify areas for improvement, and contribute to a more collaborative writing process.
8. **Customised Reading Experiences:** AI's analytical capabilities allow for the customisation of the reading experience based on user behaviour and preferences. This includes tailoring the structure, tone, and format of content to suit individual reader preferences.

9. **Market Trends and Insights:** AI's data analysis prowess can identify market trends, helping writers stay informed about popular topics and reader preferences. This valuable insight informs content strategy and ensures relevance.

Projections forecast a substantial rise in the use of generative AI for content creation, with estimates predicting a 54 per cent growth in adoption over the next few years. This anticipated increase highlights the growing impact of generative AI in the content writing field. As we leverage these advancements, it is crucial for writers to address the ethical and legal issues that arise to maintain a balance between AI's capabilities and their own creative expression. These considerations will be explored in the following section.

Legal Vulnerabilities and Copyright Issues

So far, we have examined the remarkable rise of generative AI and its transformative potential. However, this advancement brings with it significant challenges and ethical concerns. Issues such as biases in training data, the risk of spreading misinformation, and the necessity for transparency in AI-generated content highlight the need for careful consideration. As we move forward, finding a balance between innovation and responsibility is crucial. In the following section, we will address some of the key legal and copyright issues that must be navigated to ensure the ethical and effective use of AI in content creation.

One of the primary legal concerns regarding AI-generated content is the issue of ownership and rights. A March 2023 survey of brand marketers in the United States highlighted this, revealing that while 45 per cent of respondents were most concerned about the high costs of AI implementation, 41 per cent also expressed worries about legal vulnerabilities and data privacy issues. This indicates that legal and ethical considerations are almost as critical as the financial aspects when integrating AI into content creation. Moreover, as AI systems generate content autonomously, determining authorship and ownership becomes complex. This issue is compounded by the fact that, although AI systems are trained on extensive datasets, they may inadvertently reproduce content that closely resembles copyrighted material. This raises complex questions about ownership rights—whether they belong to the user, the developer, or the AI itself—and presents challenges in complying with intellectual property laws. Without clear frameworks for defining ownership and rights, there is a risk of legal disputes and potential repercussions for creators. Additionally, as AI-generated content becomes more prevalent, issues related to plagiarism and the use of copyrighted material without proper attribution become paramount. Establishing well-defined guidelines and maintaining ethical standards in content creation is crucial to upholding the integrity of the creative process and respecting the intellectual property of others.

Another critical issue to address is data privacy, emphasising the need for stringent measures to protect user data used in training AI models. As AI systems learn from diverse datasets, ensuring that sensitive or personally identifiable information is handled responsibly is vital to fostering trust among users.

In conclusion, the rise of generative AI in content creation is unstoppable, making it essential to address legal vulnerabilities and copyright issues proactively. Developing robust frameworks for ownership, respecting copyright laws, and maintaining data privacy are crucial for harnessing AI's potential responsibly and ethically.

However, the question remains: how can we balance innovation with legal and ethical considerations in this rapidly evolving industry? This is a critical challenge that we will explore in the next section, where we will discuss strategies and best practices for navigating the intersection of technological advancement and regulatory compliance.

Navigating Legal Challenges in Generative AI Content: A Rubric-Based Approach

As discussed earlier, due to the legal vulnerabilities associated with generative AI content, it is crucial to carefully edit and review the material before sharing it on any digital platform. Notably, there are 16 rubrics available for measurement, and each rubric constitutes a dedicated chapter. This organisational structure allows you to navigate seamlessly between sections or prioritise chapters based on your specific interests.

Before we explore the 16 rubrics for editing, let me clarify the purpose of this application. My aim is to organise these rubrics into three sections: Accuracy, Refinement, and Customization. This will allow for better management and application of each rubric to specific aspects of content editing. Moreover, the simplification of the process at the end of the book will streamline the editing workflow, making it more efficient and accessible for readers.

I encourage you to read the book, understand the rubrics along with the examples provided, and later utilise the checklist while editing your content. For your convenience, the checklist can be downloaded from the website, and a QR code is provided at the end of this book. Simply scan it to access the checklist.

With this, we are ready to embark on this journey into the uncharted territory of generative AI, where words become a canvas for algorithms, and editors wield the pen that shapes the future of communication.

Part I
Accuracy

1
Spelling and Grammar

Having worked extensively with students preparing for English proficiency exams, I have gained invaluable insights into the nuances of effective writing. And as an English language trainer with a background in essay editing, I have retained a profound understanding of the rubrics used to assess IELTS essays. The four key parameters of assessing the IELTS writing tasks are:

1. Task Achievement/Response
2. Lexical Resources
3. Coherence and Cohesion
4. Grammatical Accuracy

I believe these parameters are essential pillars for effective content, forming the core of this book.

So, when I was structuring the rubrics for editing generative AI content, I carefully considered whether to include spelling and grammatical issues that often disrupt the flow and clarity of writing. These issues have been a recurring problem among students during my four-year tenure as an IELTS and PTE trainer, persisting regardless of their backgrounds, whether from English medium or vernacular language education. Additionally, I have encountered AI-generated web content with flawless spelling and grammar, yet the syntax failed to convey a meaningful message. This highlights the importance of not only correct language usage but also coherent and purposeful communication.

This chapter is crucial for content creators, providing essential guidance on editing content with precision and perfection. By mastering these editing techniques, creators can enhance the quality and impact of their work, maintaining professionalism and clarity throughout their content.

Strategies for Improving AI-Generated Content

The biggest myth regarding generative AI is that it can completely handle spelling and grammar without issue. Despite AI's design to produce high-quality text, it often generates sentences that lack coherence. For instance, consider this Instagram caption created by a generative AI tool:

> 'Blue unicorns tap dance gracefully on pixelated rainbows while sipping quantum lemonade made from algorithmically grown lemons in the cyberspace meadow of perpetual conversion rates.'

Is the line creative? Absolutely. Does it reference the digital space? Metaphorically, yes. Is it grammatically correct? Certainly. But does it convey a meaningful message? No, it says nothing of substance. This example illustrates that while AI can produce grammatically accurate and imaginative content, it doesn't always ensure that the text is meaningful or relevant.

Imagine if I had simply copied and pasted this caption—it could have damaged the company's image and cost me my job. For context, the prompt given was: 'Write a concise Instagram caption that shows how digital space is the only way of marketing to have maximum conversion rate if we know the right algorithms. Make it witty like a unicorn in the sea of horses.'

While the AI-generated caption was creative and grammatically correct, it missed the mark in delivering a clear, relevant message. This highlights the importance of human oversight in ensuring that AI-generated content aligns with the intended message and purpose.

An important point to note is that while AI excels at placing each part of speech correctly to avoid syntax errors, it may still produce content that lacks meaningful substance. To ensure that AI-generated text conveys a coherent and relevant message, you need to refine and improve your prompts. There are many videos, blogs, and free guides available online that offer tips for crafting better prompts. However, this book focuses on editing AI-generated content rather than prompt generation.

Therefore, it is essential to scrutinise AI-generated content to achieve top-notch writing. Start by using helpful tools like grammar checkers, but don't rely on them exclusively. Delve deeper by manually proofreading each sentence to catch errors that automated checks might miss. Additionally, seek feedback from peers—this second set of eyes can be invaluable in refining your content. Staying updated with the latest language trends and grammar rules is also crucial. Consider style guides your trusted allies in this ongoing journey to master effective writing.

Another effective technique is to read your work out loud. This simple practice can serve as a powerful tool for uncovering errors and ensuring your writing flows smoothly. By combining these strategies—using automated checks, seeking feedback, staying updated with language trends, and refining your work through vocalisation—you establish a strong foundation for clear and precise writing.

The Five Pillars of Effective AI Content Editing

While we often assume that AI-generated content will be flawless, this is not always the case. AI content can contain subtle errors that are critical and need your attention to correct. Here are five critical elements that demand meticulous attention:

1. **Grammar Accuracy**

   It is important to scrutinise the content for grammatical accuracy. AI-generated text may occasionally produce syntactical errors or awkward sentence structures. Therefore, ensure that each sentence adheres to proper grammatical rules and maintains coherence.

   The following example highlights this aspect:

   > 'The company is expanding it's operation in foreign markets.'

   After correction, the section reads as follows:

   > 'The company is expanding its operations in foreign markets.'

5. Contextual Relevance

Examine the contextual relevance of the language used. AI might misinterpret the context, leading to grammatically correct but contextually inappropriate phrases. Make sure that the language aligns with the specific context and intent of the communication. Let's take an example to understand this better.

You need to create an Instagram caption for a video featuring a drilling machine. You provided the prompt to your chosen generative AI tool, and here is the response you received:

> 'Infinite possibilities with these drills! Unleash the power of versatile needles for any wall and screws of your choice. Watch the video for endless drilling satisfaction!'

While the caption is grammatically correct, it may misinterpret the context. A more contextually relevant caption could be:

> 'Transform your DIY projects with our drills! From sturdy walls to various screws, our video guide showcases the perfect needle for every job. Drilling can be as easy as applying butter on the bread!'

This revised caption aligns more closely with the specific context of selling drills and addresses the diverse features mentioned, ensuring more contextually relevant communication.

5. **Spelling Precision**

The generative AI will right the write spellings. Did you catch that error? Interestingly, it wasn't a machine error but rather a deliberate human choice. The good news is that we have progressed beyond the era of spell errors being a persistent issue, thanks to the seamless functionalities offered by tools like Microsoft Word and Google Docs.

Despite this advancement, I have included a category dedicated to spelling in this context. The reason behind this addition is to guarantee that the spellings align precisely with your target audience. Consider scenarios where you may need to switch between British and American spellings to cater to different audiences. This can be effortlessly achieved by specifying your preference in the prompt or by introducing an additional prompt such as 'rewrite in British English.' In summary, while technology has reduced common spelling errors, this category helps you customise and adjust your content to meet the specific linguistic preferences of your audience.

6. **Consistent Style**

AI-generated text may inadvertently adopt varied styles within a single document. Thus, it is vital to maintain uniformity in language, tone, and style to enhance readability and coherence.

Here is an example that demonstrates the importance of maintaining a consistent style:

> 'In the recent match, the Seattle Mariners faced a temporary setback, but don't be disheartened. Losses

can pave the way for future victories. Let's delve into the positives and strategies for upcoming matches. In this email, I'll discuss why the recent defeat is, in fact, an opportunity for us to shine.'

In this example, the writing style starts as a formal announcement ('In the recent match . . .') but transitions into a more conversational and motivational tone ('but don't be disheartened', 'Let's delve into the positives . . .'). To ensure consistency, it is important to maintain a uniform style throughout the email, whether it is formal or conversational, for enhanced readability and coherence.

'In the recent match, the Seattle Mariners encountered a momentary setback; however, there's no need for discouragement. Every loss presents an opportunity for future victories. Let's explore the positives and strategically plan for the matches ahead. In this email, I will elaborate on why the recent defeat is, in reality, a chance for us to showcase our strengths.'

7. **Punctuation and Sentence Structure**

   Pay close attention to punctuation usage and sentence structure. AI may struggle with nuanced punctuation rules or generate sentences that lack clarity. Verify that each punctuation mark is appropriately placed, and sentences are structured to convey ideas with precision.

   The following example illustrates the importance of punctuation and sentence structure:

> 'While positivity is generally beneficial an excess of it can lead to the denial of real issues which is not helpful at all.'

After correction, the section reads as follows:

> 'While positivity is generally beneficial, an excess of it can lead to the denial of real issues, which is not helpful at all.'

In the edited sentence, I have added a comma after 'While positivity is generally beneficial' and 'denial of real issues' to enhance readability and convey a clearer connection between the clauses. This adjustment improves the sentence structure and ensures that the ideas are presented with precision. Such issues can be easily corrected with Google Word or MS Word. If you want a more comprehensive tool, you might as well use Grammarly or Pro Writing Aid.

On the next page, there is a brief checklist for ensuring spelling and grammatical accuracy that can be applied to any type of content. Make sure to check off each item in the rubric on the checklist while editing content. (The full checklist is provided at the end)

Caption	**Good**	**Needs Improvement**
Grammatical Accuracy	[ ]	[ ]
Spellings for Regional Preference	[ ]	[ ]
Contextual Relevance	[ ]	[ ]
Punctuations and Sentence Structures	[ ]	[ ]
Consistent Style	[ ]	[ ]

2
Bias and Sensitivity

In January 2018, H&M faced a significant controversy following the release of an online advertisement. The ad featured a young black boy wearing a green hoodie with the text 'Coolest Monkey in the Jungle.' Almost immediately, social media erupted with criticism, condemning the choice of words, particularly the use of 'monkey.' The backlash was swift and widespread, with customers, celebrities, and activists expressing their concerns about the racially insensitive nature of the advertisement. The association of a black child with language that historically had been used as a racial slur intensified accusations of racism against H&M.

In response to the mounting criticism, H&M issued an apology. The company acknowledged the valid concerns raised by the public and clarified that it was not their intention to offend or perpetuate racial stereotypes. Despite the apology, the incident had a lasting impact on H&M's reputation, highlighting the importance of sensitivity and cultural awareness in marketing campaigns, especially in the era of social media where such controversies can quickly escalate.

The H&M marketing controversy offers a crucial lesson for content writers about the paramount importance of cultural sensitivity in language and messaging. It underscores the need for a thorough review process, ensuring that content does not inadvertently perpetuate stereotypes or offend specific communities. This aspect is essential in all content creation fields, particularly in advertising and marketing. Here, it is even more important to understand the potential impact of words, phrases, and visual elements, especially in a globalised context where campaigns can reach diverse audiences.

Moreover, it is vital to recognise that the lesson extends beyond just avoiding overtly discriminatory language. It also involves understanding cultural nuances, historical sensitivities, and how different communities might interpret the content. Collaborative efforts that involve individuals from different cultural backgrounds can contribute to a more inclusive and culturally aware approach to content development. Additionally, instituting comprehensive reviews and checks for potential sensitivities in language can help mitigate the risk of unintentional offensiveness in marketing and advertising campaigns.

Bias and Sensitivity in AI-Generated Content

One of the reasons generative AI can produce biased or sensitive responses is indeed linked to the data it has been trained on. If the training data contains biases or sensitive content, the AI model can inadvertently learn and replicate those patterns in its responses. This emphasises the importance of regularly reviewing and refining the training data to minimise unintended biases and sensitivities in the AI-generated content.

Another reason for bias in generative AI responses can be the lack of diverse and representative training data. If the data used to train the AI model is not comprehensive and does not encompass a wide range of perspectives, it may inadvertently reflect and reinforce existing biases present in that limited dataset. Diversifying and balancing the training data with respect to various demographics, cultures, and viewpoints is crucial to mitigate biases in generative AI responses.

In the next section, we will outline key points to consider when checking for biases or sensitivity issues in AI-generated content.

The Five Pillars for Ensuring Sensitivity and Inclusivity

Below is a simplified guide for editing content to address bias and sensitivity.

1. **Review Output Thoroughly**

   Carefully read through AI-generated content. Look for any language or perspectives that might be biased or sensitive. Pay close attention to how different groups, cultures, and individuals are portrayed. This involves not just superficial reading but a deep analysis of the underlying messages and assumptions in the content. Remember that AI can sometimes perpetuate subtle biases present in its training data, so it's important to be vigilant in identifying and correcting these.

2. **Check for Inclusive Language**

   Ensure the content uses inclusive language that doesn't favour any particular group, party, or community. Be mindful of gender-neutral terms and avoid stereotypes.

For example, instead of using gendered pronouns like 'he' or 'she,' consider using 'they' or rephrasing sentences to be more inclusive. Also, avoid language that could reinforce harmful stereotypes, such as assuming certain professions or roles are predominantly occupied by a particular gender or ethnicity.

3. Verify Cultural Sensitivity

Check if the content is culturally sensitive. Avoid making assumptions or generalisations about specific cultures or communities. This means recognising that cultural norms and practices vary widely and being careful not to present one culture as superior or more 'normal' than another. Whenever possible, use specific and accurate language rather than broad generalisations that might overlook the diversity within a culture.

4. Avoid Offensive Terms

Scrutinise the text for potentially offensive terms. Make sure the language used is respectful and considerate. Words that may seem neutral to some audiences can be offensive to others, so it is crucial to be aware of the potential impact of your word choices. If you are unsure about a term's appropriateness, err on the side of caution and consider using a different word or phrasing. Always prioritise language that reflects respect and empathy for all groups.

5. Consider Diverse Perspectives

Think about how different people might interpret the content. If possible, seek feedback from individuals representing various backgrounds. This can help identify any unintentional biases or insensitivities in the content. Encouraging input from a diverse group of readers can provide a broader perspective and ensure that the content is fair and inclusive for everyone. This practice not only enriches the content but also helps build trust with a wider audience.

In summary, it is important to be proactive in addressing bias and sensitivity in AI-generated content. If you take the time to review and edit your content, you can help to create a more inclusive and respectful online environment. By incorporating these steps into your editing process, you can effectively address bias and sensitivity in the AI-generated content.

Key Questions for Identifying Bias and Sensitivity in AI-Generated Content

Check for Bias	Check for Sensitivity	Additional Considerations
Does the content stereotype or generalise about certain groups of people?	Does the content use offensive or harmful language?	Is the content aligned with your organisations's values?
Does it use biased language or framing?	Does it address sensitive topics in a respectful and appropriate way?	Is it consistent with your brand voice and messaging?

Check for Bias	Check for Sensitivity	Additional Considerations
Does it exclude or marginalise certain perspectives?	Does it consider the potential impact on different audiences?	Does it meet any legal or regulatory requirements?
Does it represent a diversity of voices and experiences?	Does it avoid triggering or upsetting reactions?	Have you considered the potential for unintended consequences?
Does it reflect a variety of viewpoints?		

3
Credibility and Sources

STEPHEN GLASS, A JOURNALIST, FACED A SIGNIFICANT SCANDAL when it was uncovered that many of his articles were built upon a foundation of deception. Glass worked for publications like *The New Republic,* where he fabricated information, created fictional sources, and invented events to support his stories. His actions came to light when editors and fact-checkers discovered the extensive network of falsehoods within his work. This revelation not only led to the retraction of numerous articles but also damaged Glass's professional reputation and credibility. The incident underscored the importance of rigorous fact-checking and the need for journalists and content creators to ensure the accuracy and authenticity of their information before presenting it to the public. The fallout from Glass's deceptive practices serves as a cautionary tale about the severe consequences that can arise when foundational information lacks credibility and truthfulness.

Glass's case highlights the critical importance of fact-checking and ensuring the credibility of sources before publishing any information. While not a marketer, the lesson from this incident applies universally to content creators, journalists, and marketers alike. Providing accurate and reliable information is essential for maintaining audience trust, and any lapse in fact-checking can lead to severe consequences, including public backlash and damage to one's professional reputation.

In summary, upholding accuracy and credibility is essential for all content creators. In this chapter, we will delve into effective strategies and practices for maintaining content integrity and building trust with the audience.

The Importance of Credible AI-Generated Content

As a content creator, it is vital to ensure that AI-generated content is credible and backed by reliable sources. Here is why:

1. **Professionalism and Authority**
   Delivering credible content not only reflects your professionalism but also establishes you as a trusted authority in your field. This bolsters your reputation and distinguishes you from others. Conversely, consistently producing unreliable or unverified information can severely damage your reputation, leading to lasting negative consequences and undermining your audience's confidence in your expertise and trustworthiness.

2. **Audience Engagement**
   Well-researched and substantiated content effectively engages your audience, encouraging them to interact,

comment, and share. In contrast, content that lacks credibility is less likely to engage readers, as they are more cautious about interacting with material they perceive as unreliable.

3. **Building Trust**

Content that can withstand scrutiny positions you as a reliable source of information, reinforcing your brand's positive image and building a strong sense of trust among your audience. On the other hand, compromised credibility can lead to a loss of trust, with readers turning to more reliable sources and diminishing their confidence in your content.

4. **Relationship Building**

Trustworthy content fosters a positive relationship between you and your audience, significantly enhancing the overall trustworthiness of your brand or platform. Ignoring the importance of credibility in content creation can harm this relationship and diminish the impact and influence of your work.

5. **Adherence to Standards**

Spreading false or unverified information can lead to legal issues, potentially resulting in legal implications and damaging your professional standing. By adhering to industry standards and ethical guidelines, your content not only meets the required standards but also strengthens your ability to retain and expand your audience over time.

6. **Strategic Impact**

Ensuring content credibility is a strategic move that enhances your brand's reputation, opening doors for potential partnerships, collaborations, and growth opportunities within your industry. Conversely, a lack of credibility can hinder such opportunities, as businesses and individuals may hesitate to associate with content creators whose information is not trustworthy.

7. **Preventing the Spread of Misinformation**

In an era where misinformation is rampant, content creators have a responsibility to vet information thoroughly. Verifying sources is crucial, as readers might unknowingly consume and share inaccurate content, potentially leading to confusion and harm.

Steps to Ensure the Credibility of Generative AI Content

Ensuring the credibility of AI-generated content is crucial to maintaining trust with your audience. While AI can produce vast amounts of information quickly, it is essential to verify that the content is accurate, reliable, and up to date. Here's a straightforward guide to help you cross-check facts, validate sources, and enhance the overall trustworthiness of your AI-generated material

1. **Verify Information Accuracy**

Cross-check the information provided by the AI with reliable sources. Verify that all facts, statistics, and data are accurate and up to date. A quick Google search can help, but it is important to thoroughly read and evaluate the articles or sources recommended by Google to ensure their credibility.

Let's say your AI-generated content mentions that the Great Wall of China is over 21,000 kilometres long. To ensure accuracy, you will need to cross-check this fact with reliable sources. A quick search might lead you to a reputable site like History.com, which confirms that the wall is indeed about 21,000 kilometres long. However, don't just stop there. Look for additional sources, such as scholarly articles or official publications, to confirm that this figure is up-to-date and accurate. Sometimes, articles may contain outdated or incomplete information, so it is wise to consult multiple sources to get a comprehensive view.

2. Check Citations and References

If the AI includes specific references or citations, verify them. Also, make sure that the sources you are referring to are reputable and authoritative in the given field.

For example, if your AI content references a study on climate change published by a well-known university, you should check that the study is indeed from a reputable institution and authored by experts in the field. If the content cites a paper from the University of Oxford, verify that the study is genuine by visiting the university's website or academic databases. Ensuring that the sources are authoritative helps maintain the integrity of the content and builds trust with your audience.

3. Look for Consistency

Check if the information in the AI-generated content aligns with established knowledge in the subject area. Consistency is key to credibility.

Consider an AI-generated article discussing the benefits of a Mediterranean diet. If the content claims that this diet reduces the risk of heart disease by 50 per cent, you would want to see if this aligns with established knowledge. Checking reputable health sources like the All India Institute of Medical Sciences (AIIMS) or NHS guidelines might reveal that while the Mediterranean diet is beneficial, the exact percentage might vary. Ensuring consistency with well-established information helps avoid misleading your readers with inaccurate claims.

4. Assess Plausibility

Evaluate the plausibility of the information. If something seems improbable or lacks support, consider fact-checking or seeking additional sources.

Suppose your AI content includes a statistic stating that a certain type of fruit can cure cancer. This claim should be assessed for plausibility. A quick check with trusted medical sources, like the Indian Council of Medical Research, National Health Service (NHS), or Cancer Research UK, might show that while the fruit has health benefits, it does not have the proven ability to cure cancer. Evaluating the plausibility of such claims ensures that your content doesn't spread misinformation.

5. Utilise Fact-Checking Tools

To further ensure accuracy, you can use fact-checking tools like Snopes or FactCheck.org. These tools can quickly highlight any inaccuracies or questionable content, helping you maintain high standards of reliability. For example, if your content includes a claim about a recent political event, you might use PolitiFact to verify the accuracy of statements made by public figures.

Some of the popular fact-checking tools that can help you verify the credibility of content are as follows:

i. Snopes

Snopes is a widely recognised fact-checking website that investigates and debunks or confirms various claims, rumours, and misinformation.

ii. FactCheck.org

FactCheck.org is a nonpartisan, nonprofit organisation that monitors the factual accuracy of statements made by major US political players.

iii. PolitiFact

PolitiFact is a fact-checking website that focuses on statements made by politicians and public figures, rating them on a 'Truth-O-Meter.'

iv. Media Bias/Fact Check

Media Bias/Fact Check is a resource that provides assessments of the bias and reliability of various news sources.

v. **NewsGuard**

NewsGuard is a browser extension that rates news websites based on their credibility and transparency, helping users identify trustworthy sources.

In summary, when you incorporate these steps into your content creation process, you can enhance the credibility of AI-generated content and ensure that it meets the standards of accurate and reliable information.

Key Takeaways

1. Cross-check the information thoroughly.
2. Make sure to include the citations to give credit to the original source when required.
3. Make sure to check for plagiarism as AI churns out information that had been fed to it from already published work.

4

Factuality

THE THERANOS CASE IS A WELL-DOCUMENTED STORY that completely shook the world. Theranos was a health technology company founded by Elizabeth Holmes in 2003. The company claimed to have developed a revolutionary blood-testing technology that could detect a wide range of medical conditions with just a few drops of blood. However, as investigative journalists and regulatory authorities scrutinised Theranos' claims, it was revealed that the technology didn't work as promised, and the company had misled investors and the public about its capabilities. Elizabeth Holmes and another senior executive, Ramesh 'Sunny' Balwani, faced legal consequences, and the company eventually dissolved.

The Theranos scandal became a high-profile case highlighting the importance of accuracy, transparency, and ethical practices in business and marketing. It serves as a cautionary tale about the potential consequences of overpromising and under-delivering, emphasising the need for factual accuracy in various aspects, including content creation.

As a content creator, there are several valuable lessons to learn from the Theranos case. Firstly, the importance of fact-checking cannot be overstated. Always rigorously fact-check the information you include in your content. Ensure that any claims, statistics, or data are accurate and supported by reliable sources. Misleading or false information can damage your credibility, eroding the trust your audience places in you.

Transparency is another critical aspect. Be transparent about the content you create. If there are limitations or uncertainties, communicate them clearly. Avoid making exaggerated claims that could mislead your audience. Honesty builds trust, and transparent communication fosters a healthy relationship with your audience.

Maintaining high ethical standards is also essential. Uphold ethical principles in your content creation. Avoid using deceptive tactics or making promises that cannot be fulfilled. Ethical behaviour is crucial for long-term success and maintaining a positive reputation in the eyes of your audience. Furthermore, prioritise quality over hype. It is tempting to use sensationalism or hype to garner attention, but sustainable success comes from delivering valuable and truthful content consistently. Quality content, even if it doesn't make flashy promises, builds a more loyal and engaged audience over time.

Lastly, understand that building trust takes time. Trust is hard to earn but easy to lose. Building a trustworthy reputation takes time and effort. Consistently delivering accurate and reliable content contributes to establishing reliability and trust with your audience. Remember that these are crucial for the long-term success of your content creation endeavours.

The Importance of Accuracy in Your Content

Checking for facts in content editing is important for a few key reasons. Let's explore them.

1. Factual content ensures that the information presented is accurate and reliable. This accuracy helps build trust with your audience, as they know they can rely on your content for correct information.
2. If the facts in your content are inaccurate, it could lead to misunderstandings and confusion among your audience. Fact-checking helps prevent the spread of misinformation.
3. When you consistently provide accurate and well-researched information, it enhances your reputation and authority in your field.
4. Audiences are more likely to trust and engage with content that offers reliable information. This positive engagement fosters a good relationship between you and your readers.
5. Spreading false information can have legal consequences, so ensuring the accuracy of your content is a proactive measure.
6. Fact-checking is a responsible practice that demonstrates your commitment to delivering high-quality, truthful content.
7. Maintaining your reputation is tied to the accuracy of the information you provide. Consistent fact-checking safeguards your reputation and ensures a positive perception among your audience.

8. Having factual content empowers your readers to make informed decisions. Whether it is educational content or news, accurate information contributes to your audience's ability to make sound judgements.

Factuality Versus Credibility

While credibility and factual accuracy are related, they are not exactly the same. Credibility generally refers to the trustworthiness and reliability of the source providing the information. It involves assessing whether the source is reputable, unbiased, and has a history of providing accurate information. On the other hand, factual accuracy specifically relates to whether the information presented is true and corresponds to verifiable facts. It is possible for a source to be considered credible, yet the information it provides might still contain inaccuracies.

In your edit list, if you have already verified the credibility of the source and checked for reliable references, you have taken an important step in ensuring the reliability of the information. However, it is still advisable to check for factual accuracy, especially if the content involves specific details, statistics, or claims that can be independently verified. This additional step helps confirm that the information aligns with accurate and verifiable facts.

So, while credibility and factual accuracy are closely related, it is beneficial to treat them as distinct aspects when assessing the overall reliability of information.

Content Accuracy and Credibility Checklist

Here are key points to follow when checking for content accuracy and credibility:

1. **Fact-Checking**
    - Verify all facts, statistics, and data against reliable sources.
    - Cross-check claims with multiple reputable sources.
    - Confirm the authenticity of any quoted information or data.
2. **Transparency**
    - Clearly disclose any limitations or uncertainties in the content.
    - Avoid making exaggerated or unverified claims.
    - Communicate any potential biases or conflicts of interest.
3. **Ethical Standards**
    - Ensure that the content does not use deceptive practices or false promises.
    - Prioritise delivering valuable and truthful information over sensationalism.
    - Adhere to ethical guidelines and industry standards in content creation.
4. **Source Credibility**
    - Assess the reliability and reputation of the sources used.
    - Ensure sources are unbiased and have a history of accurate information.
    - Validate the credibility of the authors and organisations cited.

5. **Factual Accuracy versus Credibility**
    - Confirm that the information aligns with verifiable facts.
    - Distinguish between the credibility of sources and the factual accuracy of the content.
    - Perform a final review to ensure all details are correct and substantiated.

Key Takeaways

1. Always fact-check your content to ensure accuracy and maintain credibility, as misleading information can damage trust and have legal repercussions.
2. Uphold transparency and ethical standards in your content by avoiding exaggerated claims and prioritising truthful, high-quality information.
3. Understand the distinction between credibility and factual accuracy and ensure both are thoroughly checked to provide reliable and trustworthy content to your audience.

5
Thorough Analysis

ONE NOTABLE STORY THAT SHOWCASES THE POWER OF thorough analysis in content creation is the success story of the editorial team at *The New York Times,* particularly during the publication of 'The 1619 Project.' Led by journalist Nikole Hannah-Jones, the project aimed to reframe the country's history by placing the consequences of slavery and the contributions of Black Americans at the centre. The team undertook extensive research, delving into historical records, primary sources, and scholarly works to provide a comprehensive and nuanced perspective on the impact of slavery on American society. This thorough analysis allowed the editorial team to present a compelling narrative that challenged existing historical narratives and sparked crucial conversations about the nation's past.

The success of 'The 1619 Project' not only emphasised the importance of thorough analysis in content creation but also highlighted the role of editors and journalists in shaping public discourse through well-researched and thought-provoking content. This positive example illustrates how in-depth research and analysis can lead to impactful and influential storytelling, contributing to a deeper understanding of complex subjects.

Analysing AI-Generated Content

Conducting a thorough analysis of AI-generated content is imperative in our rapidly advancing technological landscape. As artificial intelligence continues to play an increasingly prominent role in content creation, it becomes essential to scrutinise the outputs generated by these systems. This meticulous examination serves several critical purposes, contributing to the responsible and ethical deployment of AI-generated content.

Let's explore the key reasons why thorough analysis is essential when dealing with AI-generated content.

1. While AI systems can exhibit impressive capabilities, they are not immune to errors. Thorough scrutiny allows us to identify and rectify inaccuracies, preventing the dissemination of misinformation. In contexts where the information is crucial, such as in news reporting or academic research, the reliability of AI-generated content must be upheld through rigorous examination.
2. Ethical considerations demand a careful evaluation of AI-generated content. Issues related to bias, fairness, and inclusivity can arise in the training data and algorithms that power these systems. A thorough analysis helps identify and address these biases, ensuring that the content produced is free from discriminatory elements and aligns with ethical

standards. This is particularly important in sensitive domains such as healthcare, finance, and criminal justice, where biased content can have significant real-world consequences.

3. A robust analysis is essential for maintaining accountability in the development and deployment of AI systems. Understanding the limitations and potential risks associated with AI-generated content allows for the establishment of clear guidelines and safeguards. This, in turn, fosters responsible usage and helps developers, organisations, and policymakers make informed decisions about the deployment of AI technologies.
4. When it comes to creative expression, a thorough analysis of AI-generated content is equally pertinent. It allows us to appreciate the artistic and creative elements while discerning the role of AI in the creative process. This nuanced understanding is crucial for acknowledging the collaboration between human creativity and machine intelligence, fostering a more informed and appreciative perspective of AI-generated content in fields like art, music, and literature.

In conclusion, careful examination of AI-generated content is indispensable for ensuring accuracy, upholding ethical standards, maintaining accountability, and appreciating the intricate dynamics between human and machine creativity. By conducting thorough analyses, we pave the way for the responsible integration of AI into various facets of our lives, mitigating potential risks and maximising the benefits of this transformative technology.

The Six Pillars of Thorough AI Content Analysis

When it comes to AI-generated content, a bit of careful scrutiny goes a long way. AI is brilliant at generating text quickly, but it doesn't always get things right. To make sure the content is both useful and reliable, it is essential to assess several key aspects of what the AI produces. By focusing on areas like context, consistency, and thematic alignment, you can ensure that the AI-generated content meets the highest standards of quality and clarity.

Let's take a closer look at six key parameters to consider while analysing the content generated by AI.

1. Understanding Context

AI models may lack a deep understanding of context, leading to content that might be misinterpreted or lack nuance. Assessing context ensures that the generated content aligns with the intended meaning and is appropriate in different situations.

Beginning by examining the prompts or queries given to the AI model, one can easily assess whether the generated content accurately responds to and understands the context of these prompts. Test the AI model's ability to adapt responses to different contextual scenarios. Ensure that the generated content remains coherent and relevant across various contexts.

2. Detecting Inconsistencies

Inconsistencies in AI-generated content can arise due to errors or lack of coherence in the training data. Detecting inconsistencies ensures that the information provided is internally coherent and does not present conflicting details.

Thus, it is important to cross-reference information within the generated content to identify potential inconsistencies. Check for contradictions or conflicting details, especially when addressing multiple aspects of a topic. Compare the generated content with reputable external sources to verify the accuracy and consistency of facts and information presented.

3. Analysing Semantic Structure

AI models may struggle with the nuanced use of language and semantic structures. Analysing the semantic structure helps identify whether the content accurately conveys the intended meaning, avoids ambiguity, and adheres to linguistic conventions.

This can be achieved by evaluating whether the generated content aligns with the overarching theme or topic. Ensure that the semantic structure contributes to a cohesive narrative or argumentation. Additionally, scrutinise the use of language and synonyms to assess the model's proficiency in conveying nuanced meanings. Address any instances where the model may misinterpret or misapply semantic elements.

4. Evaluating Logical Flow

A logical flow in content is essential for comprehension. Evaluating the logical flow ensures that ideas are presented in a coherent manner, making it easier for the audience to follow the narrative or argumentation.

To attain cohesive readability, make sure to examine the content sequentially to ensure a logical progression of ideas. Identify any breaks in logical flow or instances where the narrative deviates without proper transitions. Assess the use of transitional phrases to determine if the AI model effectively connects sentences and paragraphs, facilitating a smooth and coherent flow of information.

5. Checking for Redundancies

Redundancies in content can affect readability and may lead to information overload. Checking for redundancies ensures that the content is concise and clear and does not repeat information unnecessarily.

To address redundancies in your content, evaluate the content for unnecessary repetition or redundant information. Ensure that each element contributes meaningfully to the overall message without introducing unnecessary redundancy. Identify patterns of repetition, both in terms of wording and concepts, to eliminate redundancies and enhance the clarity of the content.

6. Assessing Thematic Consistency

Maintaining thematic consistency is crucial for conveying a unified message. Assessing thematic consistency helps ensure that the content aligns with the chosen theme or topic and does not deviate inappropriately.

Thus, it is important to confirm that the generated content consistently aligns with the central theme or topic. Identify any deviations that may compromise the thematic integrity of the information. Evaluate how well the content maintains thematic consistency throughout its progression, ensuring that each section contributes logically to the overarching theme.

In conclusion, each of these pillars addresses specific aspects of language and communication that AI models may struggle with. By systematically evaluating these elements, you enhance the overall quality and reliability of AI-generated content. This approach not only helps in producing content that is factually accurate but also ensures that it meets high standards of clarity, coherence, and relevance.

Key Takeaways

1. Check the AI-generated content thoroughly for anomalies and discrepancies.
2. Read twice to ensure the flow of information and tone consistency and eliminate any inconsistency.
3. Make sure that the content conveys the intended meaning and message effectively.

Part II
Refinement

6
Content Expansion

Neil deGrasse Tyson is a renowned astrophysicist known for making complex scientific concepts accessible to a broad audience. As an educator and science communicator, Tyson recognised the importance of reaching beyond traditional academic circles. With this in mind, he embarked on various projects, including hosting the television series *Cosmos: A Spacetime Odyssey.*

The series was designed not only to captivate science enthusiasts but also to engage viewers without a background in astrophysics. To achieve this, Tyson and his team employed visually stunning graphics, compelling storytelling, and real-world examples, transforming complex scientific ideas into digestible, entertaining, and educational content. This approach allowed a wider audience to appreciate and understand intricate astrophysical concepts, fostering a greater appreciation for science.

In content creation, expansion goes beyond simply adding more information; it involves presenting content in a way that resonates with diverse audiences. Tyson's success illustrates how a strategic approach to expanding content can bridge the gap between specialised knowledge and general understanding, making complex subjects more accessible and engaging for everyone.

Therefore, we can see that content expansion, at its core, involves the strategic enrichment of information. It goes beyond the surface, breathing life into narratives by adding depth, context, and supporting details. It is not just about saying more but about saying more meaningfully. This process is a deliberate effort to provide a comprehensive view, ensuring that the audience receives a well-rounded and informative experience.

According to a survey analysing content from various blogs, a combination of human and AI-generated content yields 5.44 times more traffic compared to relying solely on human or AI content. Statistical data also indicates that user interaction tends to be lower with AI-generated content. This underscores the importance of employing these rubrics as your toolkit to craft content that is both engaging and compelling.

The significance of content expansion lies in its ability to captivate and resonate. It transcends the limitations of brevity, allowing for a thorough exploration of ideas. In a world inundated with information, expanding content ensures that your message stands out, offering substance and value to your audience. Whether crafting a compelling story or providing in-depth insights, the impact of expanded content is undeniable. This strategy not only bridges the gap between specialised knowledge and general understanding but also highlights the critical role of enriching content. Moreover, as demonstrated by recent surveys, combining human and AI-generated content can significantly boost engagement and traffic. Therefore, adopting a thoughtful approach to content expansion ensures your message not only stands out but also delivers a lasting impact in an information-rich world.

The Role of Depth and Detail in Enhancing Content

As discussed earlier, content, when expanded thoughtfully, becomes a canvas for richer expressions. It enables the incorporation of complicated details, creating a tapestry of information that is both insightful and immersive. Think of it as adding layers to a painting, each layer contributing to the overall depth and complexity of the masterpiece.

By enhancing content depth and detail, we unlock the potential to engage diverse audiences. From elaborate storytelling to presenting comprehensive analyses, the expanded content caters to varying levels of curiosity and interest. Simply put, it is a strategic tool that empowers content creators to provide a holistic experience, leaving a lasting impression on readers, listeners, and viewers.

Let's explore these two aspects in detail and explore how we can incorporate them into our own writing.

1. Content Depth

When it comes to AI-generated content, there is a possibility that it may lack the depth and engagement needed. A free version of AI typically produces responses ranging from 300 to 500 words, suitable for concise web content. However, if you are crafting a comprehensive information manual or blog article, it is crucial to ensure that all necessary details are covered.

It is important to understand that content depth isn't merely about the amount of information provided; it is about the quality of the storytelling and the richness of the context integrated into the narrative. Think of it as a three-dimensional experience in a two-dimensional space. It involves providing additional insights, background, and perspectives that go beyond the surface-level understanding. The same concept applies to writing where the work not only presents facts but takes you on a journey, providing historical context, real-life examples, and expert opinions. This multifaceted approach enhances the richness of the content, capturing the audience's attention and fostering a deeper connection. Adding layers of information requires a strategic approach. One effective technique is incorporating relevant examples and case studies. Real-world instances not only illustrate key points but also anchor the content in relatable scenarios, making it more accessible to the audience. Another technique involves providing in-depth analyses and insights. Instead of skimming the surface, breaking down complex concepts into digestible portions. This approach caters to a diverse audience with varying levels of expertise. Additionally, storytelling is a powerful tool for creating content depth. Narratives have the innate ability to captivate and emotionally engage the audience. By weaving a compelling story around the core message, content becomes more memorable and resonant.

In conclusion, understanding the depth dimension is about recognising that content is more than information; it is an immersive experience. As content creators, embracing these techniques not only elevates the quality of our content but also ensures that our narratives leave a lasting impact on those who engage with them.

Let's take a moment to review this blog article generated by AI. Assess whether there is a need for more in-depth exploration. Kindly underline sections where you believe information could benefit from elaboration, expansion, or conversely, where it might be condensed. Additionally, identify areas where the inclusion of examples could significantly enhance reader engagement. Your insights will be valuable in refining and optimising the content.

(Kindly note no formatting in terms of spacing or paragraphing is done. The text is simply copy pasted for authenticity.)

Prompt: Write a 600-word article on the need for innovation in the agricultural industry and how design firms can help them achieve that

Generated Content:
Title: Need for Innovation in the Agricultural Industry and How Design Firms Can Help Achieve It

Introduction:

The agricultural industry is at a critical juncture, facing unprecedented challenges that demand innovative solutions. From climate change and resource depletion to a growing global population, farmers must adapt to new realities to ensure food security and sustainable practices. In this context, the need for innovation in the agricultural sector has never been more pressing. Design firms, with their expertise in problem-solving and creative thinking, play a pivotal role in helping the agricultural industry embrace change and foster sustainable growth.

Challenges in Agriculture:

- **Climate Change:** Shifts in weather patterns, extreme events, and rising temperatures pose significant threats to crop yields. Innovative solutions are required to develop resilient crops and farming practices that can withstand the impacts of climate change.
- **Resource Scarcity:** Depleting water resources, soil degradation, and the overuse of chemical fertilisers contribute to resource scarcity. Agricultural innovation must focus on sustainable practices that conserve resources while maintaining productivity.
- **Population Growth:** With the global population expected to reach 9 billion by 2050, the demand for food is escalating. Agricultural innovation is essential to increase productivity and efficiency to meet the growing demand for food.
- **Technological Gap:** Many farmers, especially in developing countries, lack access to modern agricultural technologies. Bridging the technological gap through innovation is crucial to empower farmers and enhance their productivity.

How Design Firms Can Drive Innovation:

- **Problem-Solving Approach:** Design firms bring a unique problem-solving approach to challenges in the agricultural sector. By applying design thinking methodologies, these firms can collaborate with farmers, researchers, and other stakeholders to identify key issues and develop innovative solutions.
- **User-Centred Design:** Understanding the needs and challenges faced by farmers is crucial for effective innovation. Design firms employ user-centred design principles, ensuring that solutions are practical, user-friendly, and tailored to the specific needs of the agricultural community.
- **Technology Integration:** Design firms excel in integrating cutting-edge technologies into various industries. In agriculture, this could involve the development of smart farming technologies, precision agriculture tools, and data-driven decision-making systems to optimise resource use and enhance productivity.
- **Sustainable Practices:** Innovation in agriculture must prioritise sustainability. Design firms can contribute by developing eco-friendly packaging, efficient irrigation systems, and regenerative farming practices that minimise environmental impact.
- **Collaboration and Education:** Design firms can facilitate collaboration between farmers, researchers, and industry experts. By organising workshops, training programs, and knowledge-sharing initiatives,

they help disseminate innovative practices and ensure widespread adoption within the agricultural community.

Case Studies:

- **Vertical Farming:** Design firms have played a crucial role in the development of vertical farming systems, allowing crops to be grown in controlled indoor environments. This innovation reduces the reliance on traditional agricultural land, conserves water, and enables year-round crop production.
- **Precision Agriculture Solutions:** By leveraging data analytics and sensor technologies, design firms have contributed to the growth of precision agriculture. This approach optimises the use of resources, minimises waste, and enhances overall farm efficiency.

Conclusion:

Innovation in the agricultural industry is not just a luxury but a necessity. Design firms bring a fresh perspective, creative problem-solving, and a commitment to sustainable practices. By collaborating with farmers and other stakeholders, these firms can drive the much-needed transformation in agriculture. As we face the challenges of climate change, resource scarcity, and a growing population, the role of design firms becomes increasingly vital in shaping the future of agriculture. Embracing innovation today ensures a resilient, sustainable, and productive agricultural sector for generations to come.

Here is how the same content after editing will read:

Title: Need for Innovation in the Agricultural Industry and How Design Firms Can Help Achieve It

The agricultural industry stands at a critical juncture, facing an array of challenges that demand innovative solutions. The need for innovation in agriculture has never been more pressing, with factors like population growth, climate change, and the quest for sustainable practices driving a call for transformative approaches. Amidst these challenges, design firms emerge as unsung heroes, wielding the power to revolutionise agriculture through thoughtful planning, technological integration, and sustainable design practices.

Design Firms as Architects of Agricultural Efficiency

Agriculture, once considered a traditional industry, is now witnessing a paradigm shift towards modernisation. Design firms play a pivotal role in this transformation, offering solutions that address the pain points of the agricultural sector.

One significant drawback lies in the efficient use of resources. Farms often grapple with the optimization of land, water, and energy resources. Design firms can alleviate this concern by employing precision farming techniques, optimising farm layouts, and integrating smart irrigation systems. The fusion of agricultural expertise with innovative design not only enhances productivity but also contributes to long-term sustainability.

Impact on Agricultural Innovation

A striking example of the impact of design firms on agricultural innovation is the integration of precision agriculture technologies. By leveraging GPS, sensors, and data analytics, design firms can assist farmers in making informed decisions regarding crop management. For instance, a design firm collaborated with a farming community in the Midwest to develop a precision farming solution.

The firm implemented a comprehensive plan that included the design of sensor-equipped machinery for real-time monitoring of soil conditions and crop Health. The result was a significant reduction in resource wastage, increased crop yield, and ultimately, improved profitability for the farmers. This example underscores how the synergy between agricultural knowledge and design expertise can bring tangible benefits to the industry.

Redefining Farming Practices Through Design

Beyond resource optimisation, the collaboration between design firms and the agricultural sector can lead to the development of innovative farming equipment. Traditional tools are often labour-intensive and less efficient, posing a challenge for farmers. Design firms can step in to create ergonomic and technologically advanced equipment that enhances efficiency and reduces the physical strain on farmers. This not only addresses the challenges of labour shortages but also fosters a more sustainable and modern approach to agriculture.

On a final note, the need for innovation in the agricultural industry is undeniable, and design firms emerge as key contributors to this transformative journey. The agriculture industry can thrive by optimising resources, discontinuing outdated practices, and implementing a sustainable strategy.

The integration of precision farming, smart technologies, and sustainable design principles exemplifies the potential impact of collaborative efforts between agricultural experts and design professionals.

As we cultivate innovation in agriculture, the role of design firms becomes increasingly indispensable, offering a blueprint for a more sustainable, efficient, and resilient agricultural future.

As we can see Article 1 is quite comprehensive, but it lacks a bit of flow and coherence in transitioning between sections. The points are well-organised, but the connection between how design firms can help and the case studies could be more fluid. For example, the transition from discussing the challenges in agriculture to how design firms address those challenges is somewhat abrupt. Additionally, while the content is informative, the tone is rather formal and can come across as dense, potentially making it less engaging for a wider audience.

Au contraire, Article 2 excels in readability and cohesion. It presents a more conversational and engaging tone, which makes the information more accessible. The article effectively weaves together the challenges and solutions with smooth transitions, creating a cohesive narrative. For instance, it not only introduces the challenges but immediately follows up with practical examples of how design firms have made a difference, such as the case of precision agriculture in the Midwest. This approach not only enhances the article's flow but also makes it easier for readers to connect with the content. Furthermore, Article 2's tone is more dynamic and enthusiastic, which helps in conveying the importance of design firms' contributions in a compelling way.

Overall, while Article 1 provides valuable insights, Article 2's improved readability, coherent structure, and engaging tone make it more effective in communicating the necessity and impact of innovation in agriculture.

2. Content Detail

Content detail, in the context of generative AI, refers to the meticulous attention to specifics that enhances the richness and clarity of a piece of writing. Whether you are crafting a blog article, social media caption, webpage, white paper, or case study, the depth and precision of detail can significantly impact the quality and effectiveness of your content. It involves adding elements that provide depth and specificity, making the content not only informative but also engaging and memorable for the reader.

Additionally, when discussing content detail, it is important to focus on how to make the text resonate with the audience by incorporating vivid descriptions, thorough explanations, and specific data points. This approach transforms basic content into something that can capture attention and convey authority. For instance, instead of stating that a company experienced 'significant growth,' providing detailed figures, such as 'the company saw a 45 per cent increase in revenue over the past quarter,' offers a more compelling narrative.

Let's consider an example of writing an article on the impact of AI on digital marketing. Without sufficient detail, it might look something like this:

> 'AI is changing digital marketing, and many companies are starting to use it.'

While this statement is factually correct, it lacks the necessary detail to effectively engage or inform your audience. By focusing on content detail, the revised version could be enhanced as follows:

> 'Artificial Intelligence is revolutionising digital marketing strategies, enabling companies to analyse vast amounts of consumer data with unprecedented speed and accuracy. For example, a recent study by Gartner found that 70 per cent of companies that have adopted AI tools saw a 30 per cent increase in customer engagement within the first six months. From personalised content recommendations to advanced predictive analytics, AI provides marketers with powerful tools to enhance customer experience and drive business growth.'

This expanded version not only provides specific data but also illustrates how AI impacts marketing practices, giving the reader a clearer understanding and a more engaging read.

In summary, incorporating content detail is crucial for creating high-quality, compelling content that resonates with readers, regardless of the format—be it blog articles, social media posts, or white papers. By focusing on the finer points, such as vivid descriptions and specific data, content developers can elevate their writing, making it more informative and engaging. This approach ensures that the content stands out, builds credibility, and leaves a lasting impression on the audience. Ultimately, mastering the art of content detail can significantly enhance the effectiveness of your writing, leading to better engagement and stronger connections with your readers

Next, we will explore strategies for content expansion that will elevate your narratives. The application of the following techniques promises to enrich your writing, ensuring it becomes more detailed and compelling for your audience.

i. Expanding on Ideas

Elaboration isn't merely about adding more words; it is a meticulous craft of expanding on core ideas, providing the audience with a comprehensive understanding. Think of it as unfolding a story, revealing nuanced details that contribute to the overall narrative.

To expand on an idea, rather than just stating a fact, delve into the 'why' and 'how' behind it. Unpack the complexities, explore related concepts, and provide a holistic perspective. This not only educates your audience but also keeps them engaged throughout the journey.

ii. Identifying Relevant Details for Expansion

Not all details are created equal. The key is to discern which details contribute meaningfully to the narrative. This is similar to selecting the right ingredients for a recipe—each element should enhance the overall flavour. Identify details that complement the central theme, providing valuable context and depth.

For instance, in an article about technology trends, delving into the specific applications and real-world implications of each trend adds a layer of relevance and practicality. This precision in detailed selection ensures that your content remains focused and impactful.

iii. Balancing Conciseness with Elaboration

While elaboration is essential, a delicate balance must be maintained. Avoid the pitfall of verbosity by honing the art of concise elaboration. Every word should contribute meaningfully, enhancing the reader's experience without unnecessary fluff.

Consider it as crafting a well-balanced dish—savouriness in each bite without overwhelming the palate. This balance ensures that your content remains accessible, engaging, and easy to digest.

iv. Importance of Supporting Details

Supporting details are essential in reinforcing the core message of your content. This includes providing evidence, examples, and context, lending credibility and authenticity to your narrative. Imagine these details as the foundation of a sturdy structure—they fortify your message and resonate with your audience.

v. **Avoiding Redundancy in Expansion**

Redundancy in your content is like carrying unnecessary baggage on a journey—it weighs it down and diminishes the impact. Identifying and eliminating redundant information is the first step towards crafting content that is lean, focused, and impactful. By streamlining your content, you ensure that every word serves a purpose, making your message clear, powerful, and engaging for your audience.

In essence, the techniques for elaboration and supporting details invite us to be storytellers and curators of information. By mastering these techniques, we enrich our content, making it not just informative but an immersive experience that captivates and resonates with our audience.

Now, let's examine the following example, based on the original AI-generated article titled 'Need for Innovation in the Agricultural Industry and How Design Firms Can Help Achieve It.' In this edited version, all techniques for enhancing content depth and detail have been applied to create a more comprehensive and impactful piece.

Title: Need for Innovation in the Agricultural Industry and How Design Firms Can Help Achieve It

In a rural village, the Wangari family, rooted in generations of farming, faced the stark consequences of climate change and outdated practices. Mwangi, taking over from his father, witnessed diminishing yields, erratic rainfall, and soil depletion. The community felt the strain of food shortages as traditional methods proved inadequate.

Without innovative solutions, the Wangari family and their village confronted a bleak future—depleted resources, struggling crops, and a fading agricultural legacy. The urgent need for adaptation became evident as the challenges of a changing climate threatened to erode the very foundation of their agrarian way of life.

The agricultural industry stands at a critical juncture, facing an array of challenges that demand innovative solutions. The need for innovation in agriculture has never been more pressing, with factors like population growth, climate change, and the quest for sustainable practices driving a call for transformative approaches. Amidst the challenges faced by the Wangari family, design firms emerge as unsung heroes, wielding the power to revolutionise agriculture through thoughtful planning, technological integration, and sustainable design practices.

Design Firms as Architects of Agricultural Efficiency

In the ever-evolving landscape of agriculture, design firms stand as architects of efficiency, orchestrating a crucial transformation from tradition to modernisation. Their role extends beyond aesthetics, delving into the intricate challenges faced by the agricultural sector.

A prominent challenge revolves around the judicious use of resources. Farms, both large and small, grapple with optimising land, water, and energy. Design firms, armed with a blend of agricultural expertise and innovative design, become catalysts for change. Precision farming techniques, curated farm layouts, and the integration of smart irrigation systems emerge as solutions that redefine efficiency on the agricultural canvas.

Consider the potential of integrating these solutions on a broader scale. Through collaborative efforts between agricultural experts and design firms, a new era of resource-efficient and sustainable farming practices could be ushered in. This modern agricultural narrative envisions design firms as pivotal players, seamlessly blending agricultural wisdom with innovative design thinking. Their endeavours promise not just immediate efficiency gains but also a sustainable roadmap for the future of farming.

Impact on Agricultural Innovation

A striking example of the impact of design firms on agricultural innovation is the integration of precision agriculture technologies. By leveraging GPS, sensors, and data analytics, design firms can assist farmers in making informed decisions regarding crop management. For instance, a design firm collaborated with a farming community in the Midwest to develop a precision farming solution.

The firm implemented a comprehensive plan that included the design of sensor-equipped machinery for real-time monitoring of soil conditions and crop Health. The tangible outcomes were striking—a substantial reduction in resource wastage, a marked increase in crop yield, and, notably, enhanced profitability for the farmers. This synergy between agricultural knowledge and design expertise epitomises the potential for transformative change within the industry. It showcases how the marriage of innovative design with agricultural acumen can yield not only immediate efficiency gains but also a sustainable trajectory for the future of farming.

Redefining Farming Practices Through Design

Beyond resource optimisation, the collaboration between design firms and the agricultural sector can lead to the development of innovative farming equipment.

Traditional tools are often labour-intensive and less efficient, posing a challenge for farmers.

Design firms can step in to create ergonomic and technologically advanced equipment that enhances efficiency and reduces the physical strain on farmers. This not only addresses the challenges of labour shortages but also fosters a more sustainable and modern approach to agriculture.

On a final note, the need for innovation in the agricultural industry is undeniable, and design firms emerge as key contributors to this transformative journey. The agriculture industry can thrive by optimising resources, discontinuing outdated practices, and implementing a sustainable strategy.

The integration of precision farming, smart technologies, and sustainable design principles exemplifies the potential impact of collaborative efforts between agricultural experts and design professionals.

As we cultivate innovation in agriculture, the role of

design firms becomes increasingly indispensable, offering a blueprint for a more sustainable, efficient, and resilient agricultural future.

Key Takeaways

1. Expanding content with additional details and context can make it more engaging and informative.
2. Integrating diverse content creation methods, such as combining human and AI-generated content, enhances engagement and traffic.
3. Emphasising both depth and conciseness helps maintain content effectiveness and reader accessibility.
4. Strategic content enhancement involves focusing on areas where more information can provide added value.
5. Balancing elaboration with clarity ensures content remains impactful without overwhelming the audience.

7
Completeness

ONE OF MY STUDENTS, WHO POSSESSED EXCEPTIONAL English proficiency, found himself disheartened when he scored only band 6 in his IELTS Writing Module. He achieved an overall IELTS score of 7, with individual scores of 8 in listening, 7.5 in speaking, and 7.5 in reading. This setback was particularly frustrating for him as his dream was to immigrate to Canada, leveraging his medical qualifications.

In our subsequent meetings, he expressed deep frustration over the inconsistency between his speaking and writing scores, which led him to question the fairness of the evaluation process. As he shared his concerns, I maintained patience and empathy, seeking a comprehensive understanding of the situation. To comprehend the issue completely, I requested access to the essays he had submitted via email. Additionally, I shared his performance in past mock tests.

In an effort to provide clarity and context, I guided him through our email correspondence, where I consistently offered detailed analyses based on various criteria such as task response, coherence and cohesion, grammatical accuracy and range, and lexical resources. Through this thorough examination, a recurrent theme emerged—an imperative need to enhance his approach to task response.

In the IELTS exam, the writing task demands crafting an essay that addresses multi-dimensional questions while adhering to a specified format and word count. It became apparent that, despite his proficiency, the student tended to focus on specific aspects of the task, inadvertently neglecting other critical dimensions. This pattern drew a parallel to content creation for products and services, where omitting crucial information results in an incomplete narrative. Just as an incomplete essay compromises its efficacy in an exam, incomplete content fails to deliver the desired impact and conversions in marketing scenarios.

In this chapter, we will explore how completeness in content creation mirrors the challenges faced in tasks like IELTS writing. A thorough examination of all task dimensions and a comprehensive narrative reveal strategies to ensure content is fully developed and impactful. Whether it is enhancing marketing materials or crafting compelling essays, understanding and implementing the principles of completeness will help you deliver content that meets objectives and engages your audience effectively.

Completeness in AI-Generated Response

In simple terms, the concept of completeness encapsulates the thoroughness of an AI-generated response. It is about providing users with not just accurate information but a full, well-rounded understanding of the topic at hand. Therefore, as content creators and editors, it is crucial to recognise the importance of completeness in delivering valuable and satisfying interactions.

This becomes especially challenging when AI is tasked with interpreting multiple instructions within a single prompt. Despite the instruction being concise and precise, it tends to mimic human behaviour, occasionally overlooking parts of the prompt. For instance, in the middle of a formal, conversational-toned letter, you might even come across a sudden, casual remark. This phenomenon highlights an intriguing aspect: AI, too, seems to exhibit its own form of mood swings. To achieve completeness in AI-generated responses, it is crucial to provide users with a thorough and satisfying experience. Recognising and addressing these challenges enhances the effectiveness of AI in delivering well-rounded and coherent content.

In the next section, we will review all the necessary steps to ensure that AI has addressed everything you have requested.

The Completeness Checklist: Steps to Achieve Thoroughness in AI Content

Ensuring the completeness of AI-generated content is imperative for delivering comprehensive and informative responses. The key steps involved in the process are as follows:

1. Check that all sections of the prompt are adequately addressed to ensure that the AI has comprehensively covered the intended topic or question. This step serves as a crucial checkpoint to verify that no key aspect has been inadvertently overlooked, providing assurance that the content is both relevant and accurate.

2. Scrutinise the inclusion of supporting ideas and examples. A well-rounded response not only directly answers the query but also enriches the content with relevant details, examples, or evidence. This additional layer of information not only enhances the overall quality of the content but also contributes to a more engaging and convincing narrative.

All in all, by emphasising completeness in terms of both prompt coverage and the incorporation of supporting elements, the editing process ensures that AI-generated content is not only accurate but also thorough and compelling.

To understand these two points, let's take an example.

Prompt: I want to email the subscribers about the upcoming webinar on 'Intermittent Fasting Benefits' (Speaker Mr Mario Puzo). The email must be in a casual tone encouraging people to get on with their weight loss program. You must write this email with the subject line and body part, also make sure that the call-to-action is quirky.

AI-Generated Response:

Subject: 🌟 Unlock Your Best Self: Join Our Intermittent Fasting Webinar! 🌈

Hey [Subscriber's Name],

Hope this email finds you in high spirits and ready for some exciting news! 🎉

Guess what? We're thrilled to invite you to our upcoming webinar on 'Intermittent Fasting Benefits!' 🌿✨ If you've been contemplating jumping on the weight loss wagon, this is your golden ticket to a healthier, happier you.

Why should you consider intermittent fasting, you ask? Well, imagine a lifestyle where you can devour that occasional slice of pizza guilt-free and still shed those extra pounds! 🍕💪 Our expert speakers will spill the beans on how intermittent fasting can be your secret weapon in the battle against those stubborn inches.

Here's a sneak peek of what you can expect:

🌟 Uncover the science behind intermittent fasting—it's more than just skipping meals!

□ Discover how to boost your metabolism without breaking a sweat (literally).

□♀ Learn practical tips to make intermittent fasting a breeze in your busy schedule.

Ready to kickstart your weight loss journey? RSVP now and be a part of this transformative experience! Click [Here] to secure your spot. Trust us; your future self will thank you! 🚀

P.S. We've got a surprise waiting for our early birds! 🎁 Don't miss out on the chance to snag some exclusive goodies. The early worm gets the perks, after all!

Can't wait to virtually meet you at the webinar!

Best,
[Your Name]
[Your Title]
[Your Company]

At first glance, the response in the example appears excellent. The language is encouraging, the email format—salutation, details, call-to-action, closing—is well-executed, and the subject line is witty. However, it is important to note that the response is incomplete and requires more thorough editing.

The first issue is that the speaker's name, although mentioned in the prompt, is missing. We should also include some details about the speaker to establish credibility, even though this was not specified in the prompt. Additionally, the email format needs a complete overhaul. Using emojis is outdated; modern emails are clean, highly customised, and free of emojis. In fact, emojis can sometimes trigger spam filters. Furthermore, the prompt requested a quirky call-to-action, which the AI overlooked. The call-to-action should be placed at both the beginning and end of the email, and it needs to be rewritten to be quirky and engaging.

Let's revise the email by addressing these issues and incorporating a quirky call-to-action.

Subject: Unlock Your Best Self: Join Our Webinar on Intermittent Fasting Benefits!

Hey [Subscriber's Name],

I hope this email finds you well! We're excited to share some fantastic news with you—our upcoming webinar on 'Intermittent Fasting Benefits' is just around the corner, and we want you to be a part of it!

Ready to Unleash the Inner Superhero in You? Click [Here] to Secure Your Cape . . . Uh, We Mean Spot!

In a world filled with fad diets and confusing weight loss strategies, intermittent fasting stands out as a practical and effective approach. Our expert speaker, Mr Mario Puzo, will dive into the science behind it, revealing how you can achieve your weight loss goals without stress.

Here's what you can expect:

1. Uncover the science behind intermittent fasting—it's more than just skipping meals!
2. Discover how to boost your metabolism without breaking a sweat (literally).
3. Learn practical tips to make intermittent fasting a breeze in your busy schedule.

Who is Mr Mario Puzo?

With a robust educational foundation in nutrition and esteemed certifications from leading organizations such as the Academy of Nutrition and Dietetics, Mr Mario Puzo is a seasoned expert in the field. He brings forth practical experience in guiding individuals through impactful intermittent fasting strategies, skillfully combining evidence-based knowledge with effective communication and an empathetic client-centric approach. Mr Puzo is dedicated to delivering personalised insights and fostering holistic health, backed by a proven track record of client success stories.
Trust him to be your reliable guide on your journey to unlocking the benefits of intermittent fasting.

And here's the quirky part—because who said weight loss can't be fun? The early bird gets the perks, so don't miss out on some exclusive goodies for our first registrants. Trust us; your future self will thank you!

Revitalise Yourself: Click Now!

Can't wait to virtually meet you at the webinar!

Best,
[Your Name]
[Your Title]
[Your Company]

The email in the above example is now complete. It successfully balances a persuasive tone with a friendly and engaging style. By providing clear and informative details about the webinar, the email creates a sense of excitement and highlights the value for the reader. Furthermore, the use of the quirky call-to-action adds a playful touch, making the registration process more memorable. It also introduces the speaker with credentials and helps build credibility and trust. The structured format with clear points on what participants can expect from the webinar enhances the persuasive nature of the email. The repetition of the call-to-action at the beginning and end reinforces the urgency, encouraging prompt registration. Overall, it strikes a good balance between being informative and enticing, likely encouraging subscribers to consider attending the webinar.

Key Takeaways

1. Verify that every part of the prompt is addressed fully, ensuring the AI has covered all aspects of the request.
2. Include supporting details and examples to enrich the content and make it more engaging.
3. Pay attention to the formatting and style guidelines relevant to the task; make sure the content adheres to contemporary standards and avoids outdated elements like excessive emojis.
4. Review the call-to-action to ensure it is both quirky and engaging and incorporate it effectively throughout the content to enhance reader response.

8
Tone Appropriateness

One notable example of advertising missteps occurred in 2017 when Pepsi's campaign featuring Kendall Jenner sparked widespread controversy. The advertisement attempted to tap into social and political movements, depicting a protest scene where Jenner hands a can of Pepsi to a police officer, seemingly diffusing tensions and promoting unity. However, the commercial was criticised, turning what was intended to be a unifying message into a public relations scandal.

The issue with the ad arose from its tone-deaf approach to serious social issues, trivialising the significance of real-life protests and movements. The attempt to co-opt activism for commercial gain was met with widespread backlash, as viewers perceived the ad as insensitive and an oversimplification of complex issues. The marketing effort, instead of fostering unity, was criticised for its lack of understanding and the inappropriate use of social justice themes.

This example emphasises the importance of being mindful of the tone used in marketing content, especially when addressing sensitive topics. It underscores the need for a nuanced and empathetic approach to avoid causing offence and, ultimately, damaging the brand's reputation.

Tone Appropriateness in Generative AI Content

Let's explore why it's essential to check and edit AI-generated content to ensure the tone is appropriate.

1. The inherent nature of AI may result in a lack of sensitivity to the intended tone of communication. By reviewing and adjusting the tone, you can ensure that the content aligns with the desired level of formality, professionalism, or informality, depending on the context and audience.
2. Tone plays a significant role in effective communication. A well-crafted tone enhances the overall user experience, making the content more relatable and engaging. Inappropriately formal or informal tones can impact the perceived credibility and professionalism of the content, potentially affecting how it is received by the audience.
3. Tailoring the tone to match the intended communication style helps in maintaining consistency across different pieces of content or within a specific brand voice. A consistent tone contributes to brand identity, fostering a sense of familiarity and trust with the audience.

In summary, editing for tone appropriateness is essential to ensure that AI-generated content resonates well with the audience, maintains a consistent brand voice, and effectively communicates the intended message in a manner that aligns with the context and purpose of the content.

In the next section, we will dive into the key steps to consider when assessing tone appropriateness.

Understanding Tone: Essential Considerations for Content Analysis

Crafting content with the right tone is a powerful tool that can greatly enhance its impact on readers or the target audience. Whether the content is a comprehensive long-form piece or a concise short-form message, the tone remains a consistent factor in shaping the reader's experience, guiding their perception, understanding, and emotional response.

Here are a few ways in which an appropriate and effective tone can be beneficial:

1. **Establishing Connection**

   An appropriate tone helps build a connection between the content and the reader. When you choose a tone that aligns with the reader's expectations and preferences, content creators can foster a sense of rapport and empathy. This connection makes the audience feel acknowledged and valued, which is crucial for engagement. For instance, a friendly and conversational tone in a blog post can make readers feel as if they are having a one-on-one discussion with the author, enhancing their sense of connection and personal investment in the content.

2. **Enhancing Comprehension**

   The right tone contributes significantly to clarity and comprehension. Tone can guide how information is perceived, making complex or technical content more accessible. A tone that is clear, concise, and straightforward helps ensure that the message is communicated effectively, reducing the risk of misinterpretation. For example, a professional and educational tone in an instructional manual can make technical details easier to understand, while a casual tone might simplify complex ideas for a broader audience.

3. Building Trust

A well-chosen tone establishes trust with the audience by conveying authenticity and credibility. When the tone is consistent with the content's purpose and the audience's expectations, it enhances the perceived reliability of the information presented. For instance, a serious and authoritative tone in a financial advisory piece helps build confidence in the accuracy and reliability of the advice given, fostering a sense of trustworthiness and professionalism.

4. Encouraging Engagement

Readers are more likely to engage with content that resonates with them on a personal level. An appropriate tone can make content more relatable and inviting, encouraging active participation and involvement. For example, a humorous and light-hearted tone in a social media post can stimulate interactions such as likes, shares, and comments, while an empathetic tone in a customer service email can prompt more meaningful responses and dialogues.

5. Eliciting Emotional Response

The tone establishes the emotional foundation of the content, shaping how readers feel as they engage with the message. Whether the goal is to inspire, motivate, or evoke empathy, the right tone enhances the emotional impact, making the content more compelling. For instance, a passionate and motivating tone in a fundraising campaign can stir feelings of urgency and generosity, driving readers to take action and support the cause.

6. Tailoring to the Audience

Adapting the tone to match your target audience is essential for effective communication. An appropriate tone resonates with the audience's preferences, demographics, and expectations, ensuring the content speaks directly to their interests and needs. For example, a formal and technical tone might be suitable for a professional audience in an industry report, while a casual and approachable tone would be more effective for a general audience in a lifestyle blog.

7. Fostering Memorability

Content that resonates deeply tends to be memorable. Using the right tone enhances this memorability, making it more likely that readers will remember and reference the message in the future. A tone that captures the essence of the message and aligns with the audience's emotional state can leave a lasting impression, ensuring that the content stands out and is recalled long after it has been read.

Ultimately, the tone is the subtle yet powerful thread that ties together all aspects of effective communication, making your content not only informative but also deeply meaningful. Thus, as content creators, mastering the right tone in content creation is not just about setting the mood but about strategically guiding the reader's entire journey through your message.

Three Essential Factors for Tone Tuning

The tone in AI-generated content plays a crucial role beyond just syntax and semantics; it carries the emotional depth that makes the content truly resonate with users. By setting the mood and conveying a distinct atmosphere, tone transforms mere information into a meaningful experience. It acts as the heartbeat of the content, infusing life and character into the words.

When editing generative AI content for tone appropriateness, consider the following three key factors:

1. **Audience Understanding**

Understanding your audience involves delving into their demographics, preferences, and cultural context. This means recognising their age, profession, interests, and any other factors that might influence how they perceive and interact with your content.

For instance, if your content is directed at a professional audience, such as business executives or industry specialists, adopting a formal and business-like tone is appropriate. This includes using industry-specific jargon, maintaining a serious and respectful tone, and focusing on delivering clear, concise, and actionable information. Conversely, if the content is aimed at a younger audience, such as students or young professionals, a more conversational and casual tone may be fitting. This could involve using contemporary language, engaging in a friendly manner, and incorporating humour or informal expressions to connect with the audience on a personal level.

By understanding your audience, you can craft content that resonates with them, makes them feel valued, and ultimately drives engagement. It ensures that the tone aligns with their expectations and enhances their overall experience with the content

2. Contextual Relevance

Assessing the context in which the content will be consumed is crucial for determining the appropriate tone. Different contexts require different tonal approaches to effectively communicate the message and achieve the desired impact.

For example, a social media post typically benefits from a more relaxed and conversational tone. This environment encourages engagement through casual interactions and personal connections, so a tone that is upbeat, friendly, and relatable can help capture attention and prompt responses. On the other hand, a formal report or academic paper necessitates a serious and authoritative voice. In these cases, the tone should reflect professionalism, precision, and thoroughness, providing clear and objective information without unnecessary embellishments.

Understanding the context involves considering factors such as the medium (e.g., blog, email, report), the purpose of the content (e.g., to inform, persuade, entertain), and the expected reaction from the audience. By aligning the tone with the context, you ensure that the content is appropriate for its setting and effectively serves its intended purpose.

3. Consistency with Brand Voice

Maintaining consistency with the established brand voice is essential for reinforcing brand identity and building a stronger connection with the audience. The tone of AI-generated content should align with the overall image and identity of the brand it represents, whether it is a corporate entity, a personal brand, or a publication.

For instance, if a company's brand voice is characterised by friendliness, customer-centricity, and approachability, then the AI-generated content for that company should reflect these qualities. This involves using a tone that is warm, engaging, and supportive, consistent with the brand's values and messaging. Similarly, if a brand's voice is formal, authoritative, and professional, the content should adopt a tone that mirrors these attributes, maintaining a high level of professionalism and credibility.

All in all, if you keep these factors in mind, you can ensure that the tone of the AI-generated content is appropriate for the intended audience and aligns seamlessly with the established brand voice. This approach enhances the effectiveness of the content and promotes better engagement with the readers.

Let's now consider an example of how to edit AI-generated content for tone appropriateness.

AI-Generated Response:

In a world permeated with ceaseless distractions and escalating demands on our time, the mastery of productivity has become increasingly pivotal. Whether you are an entrepreneur, a student, or a seasoned professional, discovering effective strategies for time management, overcoming procrastination, committing to tasks, avoiding distractions, and sustaining motivation can profoundly elevate your efficiency. Within this comprehensive guide, we will explore innovative approaches designed to enhance your productivity.

1. **Time Management Mastery**

   The bedrock of productivity lies in effective time management. To refine this skill, consider adopting the Pomodoro Technique, breaking your work into concentrated intervals (typically 25 minutes) followed by short breaks. Tools such as the Pomodone app seamlessly integrate this technique into your workflow, ensuring optimal productivity without succumbing to burnout.

2. **Procrastination: The Art of Defeat**

   Overcoming procrastination necessitates a nuanced understanding of its origins. Apply the 'Two-Minute Rule'—if a task requires less than two minutes, execute it immediately. Additionally, leverage the Eisenhower

Matrix to prioritise tasks based on urgency and importance. This structured approach aids in conquering procrastination by deconstructing complex projects into manageable steps.

3. Commitment Strategies

Committing to your goals forms the bedrock of productivity. Implement the 'Seinfeld Strategy,' where consistent daily actions construct a chain of success. Visualisation techniques, such as creating a vision board or maintaining a goal journal, serve as potent reminders of your commitments, fortifying your determination.

4. Distraction-Free Zones

In the era of ubiquitous digital distractions, establishing dedicated distraction-free zones is imperative. Utilise website blockers like Cold Turkey or StayFocusd to restrict access to distracting websites during work hours. Additionally, apps like Forest incentivise focus by cultivating virtual trees that wither if distractions prevail.

5. Motivation Unleashed

Sustaining motivation is an enduring challenge, but diversifying approaches can prove effective. Implement the 'Power of Three' rule, concentrating on three key tasks each day to prevent overwhelm. For an added morale boost, employ motivational apps like Fabulous or Habitica, transforming productivity into a rewarding game where task completion earns points and unlocks achievements.

6. Mindfulness and Productivity

Mindfulness techniques, encompassing meditation and deep breathing, can significantly enhance productivity. The Headspace app provides guided meditations tailored for various life aspects, including work and focus. Integrating mindfulness into your routine fosters clarity, diminishes stress, and reinforces your ability to concentrate on the tasks at hand.

7. Automation Advantages

Embrace automation to streamline repetitive tasks and liberate valuable time. Tools like Zapier facilitate seamless integration between diverse apps, automating workflows. Whether managing email responses, updating social media, or handling data entry, automation ensures efficiency, enabling you to channel your energy towards more intricate and creative endeavours.

8. Prioritising Personal Well-being

Recognising the significance of personal well-being is integral to sustained productivity. Adequate sleep, regular exercise, and a balanced diet significantly contribute to cognitive function and focus. Apps such as Sleep Cycle or MyFitnessPal can assist in monitoring and optimising these essential aspects of your life.

9. Continuous Learning for Continuous Productivity

Staying at the forefront of productivity mandates a commitment to continuous learning. Explore online courses, webinars, and podcasts centring on productivity and time management. Platforms such as Coursera, Udemy, or TED Talks offer a wealth of insights, providing fresh perspectives and actionable strategies to elevate your efficiency.

Conclusion

In the ever-evolving realm of productivity, the key lies in adopting a dynamic approach. By assimilating fresh techniques, leveraging innovative tools, and maintaining a commitment to personal growth, you can unlock your full potential. Remember, productivity is a journey, not a destination. Implement these insights, remain adaptable, and observe as your efficiency scales new heights, revolutionising the way you work and live.

In this article, examine the potential for improving tone and review the suggested adjustments provided below. Once you have compiled your observations, compare them with these recommendations to ensure tone appropriateness.

The sentence 'Whether you are an entrepreneur, a student, or a seasoned professional . . .' aims to be inclusive, but the complexity of the sentence might hinder readability. Simplifying the sentence ensures that the content remains inclusive while making it more accessible to a wider audience.

The mention of specific app names like 'Cold Turkey,' while relevant, introduces a slightly informal tone. In a professional context, using more universally recognised terms for website blockers can maintain a consistently formal atmosphere throughout the content.

While maintaining a formal tone, it is essential to strike a balance that engages the target audience. Adjusting certain expressions ensures that the content remains professional while still being engaging and relevant to your target audience.

Based on these points, the necessary changes have been made to the article. You can find the updated version below.

(Kindly note that the revisions focus solely on tone improvement and do not address other parameters discussed in previous chapters.)

Title: Enhancing Productivity: Unveiling Effective Strategies, Tips, and Tools for Maximum Efficiency

Introduction

In a world filled with perpetual distractions and increasing demands on our time, achieving mastery in productivity has become more crucial than ever. Regardless of your role—be it as an entrepreneur, a student, or an experienced professional—discovering effective strategies for time management, conquering procrastination, dedicating to tasks, averting distractions, and sustaining motivation can significantly elevate your efficiency. This comprehensive guide explores innovative approaches designed to enhance your productivity.

1. **Time Management Mastery**

   The foundation of productivity lies in effective time management. To refine this skill, consider adopting the Pomodoro Technique, breaking your work into concentrated intervals (typically 25 minutes) followed by short breaks. Tools like the Pomodone app seamlessly integrate this technique into your workflow, ensuring optimal productivity without succumbing to burnout.

2. Procrastination: The Art of Defeat

Overcoming procrastination requires a nuanced understanding of its origins. Apply the 'Two-Minute Rule'—if a task takes less than two minutes, execute it immediately. Additionally, leverage the Eisenhower Matrix to prioritise tasks based on urgency and importance. This structured approach aids in conquering procrastination by deconstructing complex projects into manageable steps.

3. Commitment Strategies

Committing to your goals is the cornerstone of productivity. Implement the 'Seinfeld Strategy,' where consistent daily actions construct a chain of success. Visualisation techniques, such as creating a vision board or maintaining a goal journal, serve as potent reminders of your commitments, fortifying your determination.

4. Distraction-Free Zones

In the age of ubiquitous digital distractions, establishing dedicated distraction-free zones is imperative. Utilise website blockers like Cold Turkey or StayFocusd to restrict access to distracting websites during work hours. Additionally, apps like Forest incentivise focus by cultivating virtual trees that wither if distractions prevail.

5. **Motivation Unleashed**

Sustaining motivation is a perpetual challenge, but diversifying approaches can prove effective. Implement the 'Power of Three' rule, concentrating on three key tasks each day to prevent overwhelm. For an added morale boost, employ motivational apps like Fabulous or Habitica, transforming productivity into a rewarding game where task completion earns points and unlocks achievements.

6. **Mindfulness and Productivity**

Mindfulness techniques, encompassing meditation and deep breathing, can significantly enhance productivity. The Headspace app provides guided meditations tailored for various life aspects, including work and focus. Integrating mindfulness into your routine fosters clarity, diminishes stress, and reinforces your ability to concentrate on the tasks at hand.

7. **Automation Advantages**

Embrace automation to streamline repetitive tasks and liberate valuable time. Tools like Zapier facilitate seamless integration between diverse apps, automating workflows. Whether managing email responses, updating social media, or handling data entry, automation ensures efficiency, enabling you to channel your energy towards more intricate and creative endeavours.

8. **Prioritising Personal Well-being**

   Recognising the significance of personal well-being is integral to sustained productivity. Adequate sleep, regular exercise, and a balanced diet significantly contribute to cognitive function and focus. Apps such as Sleep Cycle or MyFitnessPal can assist in monitoring and optimising these essential aspects of your life.

9. **Continuous Learning for Continuous Productivity**

   Staying at the forefront of productivity mandates a commitment to continuous learning. Explore online courses, webinars, and podcasts centring on productivity and time management. Platforms such as Coursera, Udemy, or TED Talks offer a wealth of insights, providing fresh perspectives and actionable strategies to elevate your efficiency.

Conclusion

In the ever-evolving landscape of productivity, the key lies in adopting a dynamic approach. By assimilating fresh strategies, leveraging innovative tools, and maintaining a commitment to personal growth, you can unlock your full potential. Remember, productivity is a journey, not a destination. Implement these insights, remain adaptable, and observe as your efficiency scales new heights, revolutionising the way you work and live.

Key Takeaways

1. Recognise that the tone in content is pivotal for fostering trust and evoking emotional responses.
2. Tailor the tone to suit both the target audience and the overarching brand identity.
3. Achieve a delicate equilibrium between formal and informal tones within the content.
4. When directing AI to incorporate these nuances, ensure the execution is seamless to preserve the intended impact.

9
Conciseness

Renowned writers stress the importance of conciseness in content creation. In this context, conciseness means delivering information clearly and effectively, using only the necessary words to convey a coherent message. It is similar to the art of distillation—achieving brevity without losing depth.

In today's information-saturated digital landscape, conciseness is more crucial than ever. Users increasingly value content that is direct and to the point, yet rich in depth. Concise content not only boosts readability but also elevates the overall user experience by making information more accessible and enjoyable. When users are seeking specific information or solutions, brevity enables quicker comprehension and enhances satisfaction. Therefore, content creators must master the art of balancing comprehensive information with brevity, avoiding unnecessary verbosity. This balance is vital for capturing and retaining user attention, particularly in an era where attention spans are short.

Copyblogger, a leading platform in content marketing and copywriting, perfectly embodies this principle. They emphasise that 'Effective communication is at the heart of successful content marketing,' a sentiment that guides their approach to delivering clear, insightful content devoid of unnecessary fluff. In contexts like customer support or chatbot interactions, where speed and clarity are paramount, concise responses are especially valuable. Users appreciate prompt, focused, and easily understandable information, which fosters trust and enhances their overall experience.

In this chapter, we will explore techniques for achieving conciseness, examine the challenges of excessive brevity, and discuss the iterative refinement processes needed to find the optimal balance. By navigating these aspects, content writers, editors, and developers will gain valuable insights into crafting responses that are both concise and rich in meaningful content, ultimately enhancing the user experience.

Conciseness in AI-Generated Content

Before diving into best practices and strategies for achieving conciseness in your content, let's briefly review its benefits

1. **Engagement:** People often have limited attention spans. Concise content is more likely to capture and maintain the reader's interest, leading to better engagement.
2. **Readability:** Shorter sentences and paragraphs enhance readability. This is crucial for online content, where users tend to skim rather than read every word.
3. **Clarity:** Concise content is easier to understand. It eliminates unnecessary details and ensures that the main message is clear and straightforward.

4. **Effectiveness:** Concise content is often more effective in conveying the intended message. It reduces the risk of information overload and ensures that the key points stand out.
5. **User Experience:** Users appreciate content that gets to the point quickly. Concise content respects the audience's time and delivers information efficiently.
6. **SEO Benefits:** Search engines often favour concise and well-structured content. It improves the chances of the content being ranked higher in search results.
7. **Brand Image:** Clear and concise communication reflects positively on your brand. It demonstrates professionalism and consideration for your audience.

In summary, embracing conciseness not only sharpens the focus of your message but also enhances readability and engagement. By delivering clear, to-the-point content, you ensure that your audience grasps the key points quickly and efficiently, reducing the risk of miscommunication and increasing the overall impact of your message.

Techniques for Conciseness

Ensuring that AI-generated content is concise involves implementing specific strategies. Here are actionable steps to achieve optimised content.

1. **Review AI Output**

AI-generated content often requires careful review to ensure conciseness and clarity. Start by identifying and removing redundant information that may have been unintentionally repeated by the AI. Simplify any complex or verbose sentences to enhance readability and precision. Ensure that every phrase contributes meaningfully to the overall message, maintaining coherence and avoiding unnecessary detail. This review process helps refine the content, making it more engaging and effective in delivering its intended message. Conciseness.

Here's an example to illustrate the importance of reviewing AI output for conciseness:

Original AI-Generated Webpage Content:

'Our company has a strong commitment to sustainability. We are very dedicated to implementing practices that are environmentally friendly and ensure that our operations have minimal negative impact on the environment. Our focus on sustainable practices is unwavering, and we work hard every day to ensure that all our activities are aligned with our sustainability goals.'

Reviewed and Concise Version:

'Our company is committed to sustainability and consistently implements environmentally friendly practices to minimise our impact on the environment. Our dedication to sustainability is reflected in all our operations.'

In the original content, the AI-generated text repeats similar ideas about the company's commitment to sustainability, leading to redundancy. The reviewed version eliminates repetitive phrases and simplifies the message while maintaining its core meaning. This approach makes the content more direct and impactful, ensuring the reader grasps the essential information quickly and clearly.

2. Eliminate Redundancies

Redundancies not only add unnecessary length to the content but may also dilute the impact of the key message. Moreover, in a world where attention spans are often limited, crafting concise content is especially crucial for capturing and maintaining the audience's interest. By eliminating extraneous sections, the content becomes more streamlined, making the central message stand out clearly. This approach not only enhances the reader's comprehension but also creates a more engaging and enjoyable reading experience.

To execute this step effectively, content creators should conduct a thorough review of the AI-generated material, identifying sections where information is repetitive or where sentences can be simplified without compromising clarity. Streamlining language requires a careful balance—removing unnecessary details while preserving essential information. The goal is to craft a narrative that is both concise and impactful, delivering the intended message without superfluous embellishments. Achieving this involves meticulous editing, ensuring that every phrase contributes meaningfully to the overall coherence and effectiveness of the content.

Let's understand this with an example of a LinkedIn post about gender pay inequality.

AI Response:

As we delve into the critical issue of gender pay inequality, it becomes increasingly apparent that women, despite their qualifications and expertise, often find themselves facing a breach of their civil rights when it comes to remuneration. This egregious disparity in compensation is a clear violation of the principles of equal pay for equal work. It is imperative that we collectively address this pressing concern and work towards creating a fair and just working environment for all.

Edited Version:

As we discuss gender pay inequality, it is evident that women, despite qualifications, face a breach of civil rights in compensation. This disparity violates equal pay principles. It is crucial to collectively address this concern and work towards a fair working environment for all.

In this streamlined version, unnecessary phrases are removed, and the language is streamlined while maintaining clarity. The core message about gender pay inequality and the violation of civil rights is retained in a more concise form for effective communication.

3. Prioritise Information

Prioritising information is a crucial step in refining AI-generated content to ensure it is both concise and effective. This process involves recognising that not all information carries the same weight in delivering the intended message. By prioritising, content creators can highlight the most relevant and impactful details, thereby capturing the reader's attention and enhancing their understanding.

To do this effectively, creators should first identify the key messages and central themes they want to convey. These core elements should be prominently featured, while less critical information can be condensed or omitted. The objective is to guide the reader through a streamlined narrative that emphasises the most important details, improving comprehension and making a lasting impact. Regularly referring to the core objectives during the editing process ensures a strategic approach to information prioritisation, resulting in content that is not only clear and concise but also compelling and purposeful.

Let's look at an example of how to prioritise information in an email to subscribers, which announces a new blog post and a special discount on women's apparel.

AI-Generated Email:

Dear Subscribers,

We hope this email finds you well. We are excited to inform you about our latest blog post, which highlights various updates and events. Additionally, we have a special promotion running for the next three days, offering discounts on a wide range of products, including women's apparel. Take advantage of this limited-time offer and browse through our entire collection to find exclusive deals on fashionable items. We value your continued support and look forward to your participation in this exciting opportunity.

Best Regards,
[Your Company]

Prioritised Email:

Hey,

Exciting news! For the next three days, enjoy special discounts on all women's apparel. Check out our latest blog post for details and discover exclusive deals on fashionable items. Don't miss this limited-time offer to upgrade your wardrobe. Your continued support means the world to us.

Best Regards,
[Your Company]

In the edited email, the information about the special discount on women's apparel has been prioritised and presented prominently at the beginning of the email. The details about the blog post and other updates are still mentioned but are condensed to maintain focus on the key message of the special promotion. This step ensures that subscribers quickly grasp the most crucial details about the limited-time offer right when they open the email.

4. Use Clear and Simple Language

Using clear and simple language is a pivotal step in crafting effective communication, especially in an environment where diverse audiences consume vast amounts of information daily It ensures that the message is accessible to a wide range of readers, regardless of their expertise or familiarity with the topic. This approach promotes inclusivity and engagement, allowing more people to understand and connect with the content.

To implement this approach successfully, content creators must choose straightforward and easily understandable words and phrases. Avoiding unnecessary complexity and jargon is central to this approach. This strategy is particularly important when dealing with topics that may be unfamiliar to certain segments of the audience. By choosing clarity over complexity, content creators can create content that resonates with a wider audience, ensuring that the intended message is not lost in unnecessary intricacies. Embracing simplicity in language also enhances the overall accessibility of the content, contributing to effective communication that leaves a lasting impact.

To illustrate this, let's examine a product description written for someone with no technical experience.

AI-Generated Response:

The MacBook Air boasts a Retina display with True Tone technology, offering an immersive visual experience. Equipped with the Apple M1 chip, it delivers unparalleled performance and efficiency. The SSD storage ensures fast data access, while the Magic Keyboard provides a comfortable typing experience. Additionally, the

MacBook Air supports macOS, providing access to a vast ecosystem of applications and features.

Edited Response:

The MacBook Air has a beautiful screen that adapts to your surroundings for a better view. It is super-fast and efficient thanks to the special chip inside. Your stuff loads quickly with its special storage, and the keyboard feels really nice to type on. Plus, it works with a bunch of apps and cool features.

In the simplified product description, technical terms have been replaced with more accessible language, making it easier for someone unfamiliar with Apple products to understand the features of the MacBook Air. This approach ensures clarity and facilitates a quicker understanding of the information being conveyed.

5. Utilise AI Editing

Utilising AI editing tools is a crucial step in refining content for conciseness, offering a technological advantage in streamlining language and improving overall clarity. AI editing tools, designed with a focus on conciseness, can systematically analyse written content, pinpoint redundancies, and offer valuable suggestions to enhance clarity. This is particularly beneficial for ensuring that complex ideas are communicated effectively without unnecessary verbosity, making the content more engaging and easier for readers to understand.

To employ this step effectively, content creators can integrate AI editing tools into their editing process. These tools can automatically identify wordy sentences, repetitive phrases, and areas where content can be more succinct. Content creators can then review the suggestions provided by the AI tool, incorporating relevant edits to enhance the overall conciseness of the content. The seamless integration of AI editing tools not only accelerates the editing process but also ensures that the final content aligns with the principles of clarity and brevity. Moreover, as technology continues to advance, leveraging AI in content editing becomes an invaluable strategy for content creators seeking to optimise their messaging for maximum impact and engagement.

Let's explore some popular AI editing tools, along with their key features and pricing options.

i. **Grammarly**

Features

- Grammarly is an AI-powered writing assistant that checks for grammar, spelling, punctuation, and style.
- It provides suggestions for sentence structure improvements, vocabulary enhancements, and overall writing clarity.
- Grammarly integrates with various writing platforms, including web browsers, Microsoft Word, and Google Docs.

Pricing

- Grammarly offers a free version with basic grammar and spelling checks.
- The premium version, which includes advanced writing suggestions, starts at $11.66 per month when billed annually.
- There is also a business plan with additional team collaboration features, starting at $12.50 per user per month (billed annually).

ii. Hemingway Editor

Features

- Hemingway Editor focuses on improving readability by highlighting complex sentences, passive voice, and common writing errors.
- It provides a readability grade and suggests ways to simplify sentences for clearer communication.
- The editor offers both online and desktop versions for flexibility.

Pricing

- The online version is free to use.
- The desktop app, available for a one-time purchase of $19.99, includes additional features like offline editing

iii. ProWritingAid

Features

- ProWritingAid provides an in-depth writing analysis, addressing grammar, style, and structural issues to improve the clarity and effectiveness of your writing.
- It provides detailed reports on areas such as overused words, sentence length, and readability.
- The tool integrates with popular writing platforms and includes a browser extension.

Pricing

- ProWritingAid has a free version with basic writing suggestions.
- The premium version, which unlocks advanced features, starts at $20 per month. Yearly plans offer discounted rates.

Another valuable resource that can aid in tracking your progress, setting milestones, and connecting with a community of fellow writers is NaNoWriMo. This exceptional platform is particularly effective for helping you complete your manuscript.

In summary, AI editing tools offer significant advantages to writers and content creators by automating the identification and correction of issues related to conciseness. These tools enable creators to refine their writing efficiently, ensuring that the final output adheres to principles of clarity and effectiveness through real-time feedback. Moreover, they save time and effort, allowing creators to focus on other critical aspects of their content.

6. Set Length Limits

Setting length limits for different types of content is an important step in content creation that ensures the desired level of conciseness is achieved. By establishing clear length limits, content creators provide structured guidelines that serve as a framework for maintaining brevity while effectively conveying the intended message. This approach will help your content stand out in an information-saturated environment, making it easier to engage your audience with concise and focused messaging.

Content experts like Julia McCoy and Gary Vaynerchuk emphasise the importance of concise and engaging content. While specific word counts can vary based on the platform and content type, they generally share the view that content should be as long as it needs to be to effectively convey the message and provide value. Gary Vaynerchuk often emphasises the value of micro-content for platforms like social media, where brevity is key due to limited attention spans. Short, impactful messages can perform well in such contexts. Julia McCoy, a proponent of quality over quantity, emphasises creating comprehensive content that thoroughly addresses the topic. However, she also recognises the need to maintain reader engagement, suggesting that articles in the range of 1,500 to 2,500 words can often strike a balance between depth and audience attention.

Setting word length limits is crucial when writing for different platforms and formats. For instance, platforms like X (formerly Twitter) and other social media channels impose character limits, which force content creators to condense their messages, making them brief, impactful, and more likely to be read and shared. Additionally, the type of writing—whether it's email marketing or blogging—also dictates the appropriate word count, as these formats vary significantly in their requirements. In each case, establishing word limits is a practical strategy to enhance conciseness, helping to capture and retain audience attention in a world where short, focused communication is essential. Ultimately, the ideal word count for maximum engagement depends on factors such as the content platform, audience preferences, and the nature of the content. It's essential to focus on delivering value, clarity, and relevance, ensuring that the content resonates with the intended audience.

In conclusion, content creators should tailor length limits to suit the nature of the content. Tailoring the limits based on the platform and content type ensures that the audience receives information in a digestible format. Additionally, it encourages creators to prioritise key messages, eliminate unnecessary details, and present information in a more focused manner. Adhering to established length limits not only enhances the overall conciseness of the content but also contributes to better engagement and understanding by respecting the audience's time and preferences.

7. Employ Formatting Techniques

Incorporating formatting techniques, such as bullet points and subheadings, is a vital step in content creation that significantly contributes to enhancing overall conciseness and readability. The necessity of employing these techniques arises from the recognition that modern audiences often engage with content in a fast-paced digital environment, where attention spans are limited. Breaking down complex information into digestible sections using clear and visually appealing formatting not only makes the content more accessible but also helps maintain the audience's focus.

To implement this step effectively, content creators should strategically use bullet points to highlight key details and subheadings to organise content into logical sections. Bullet points provide a quick and scannable overview, allowing readers to grasp essential information without delving into lengthy paragraphs. Subheadings, on the other hand, guide the reader through the content's structure, aiding in navigation and comprehension. Additionally, employing consistent and visually appealing formatting contributes to the aesthetics of the content, making it more appealing and user-friendly.

Utilising these formatting techniques ensures clear and concise communication of messages, allowing readers to efficiently extract valuable information while swiping through the content. This method not only resonates with the preferences of today's online audiences but also elevates the overall user experience, enhancing the content's engagement and impact. By systematically applying these steps during the editing phase of AI-generated content, you can enhance its conciseness and ensure that the final output effectively conveys the intended message in a clear and succinct manner.

Conciseness Versus Clarity

Balancing conciseness and clarity is a key challenge in generative AI responses. While brevity is crucial for effective communication, it must be paired with clarity to prevent misunderstandings. For instance, being too brief can sometimes lead to confusion, as essential details might be omitted, causing readers to misinterpret the message. Additionally, overly concise responses might lack context or nuance, making it difficult for the reader to fully grasp the intended meaning. This is particularly critical in complex subjects where the interplay of various factors needs to be conveyed comprehensively. Writers and AI systems alike must be mindful of when brevity may inadvertently introduce ambiguity.

If a response appears unclear or if there is a risk of misinterpretation, it is essential to revisit and enhance it for clarity. This involves not just expanding on the omitted details but also ensuring that the additional information is relevant and seamlessly integrated into the response. Striking a balance between conciseness and thoroughness helps in delivering information that is both precise and understandable.

Additionally, employing strategies such as providing examples, clarifying terms, and structuring information logically can help mitigate ambiguity. These techniques ensure that the response remains concise while providing enough context to prevent misinterpretation. Ultimately, the goal is to produce content that is both succinct and sufficiently informative, achieving the dual objectives of clarity and brevity.

Key Takeaways

1. Conciseness is important to deliver the desired message effectively.
2. One must avoid ambiguity while making the content concise.
3. Conciseness must ensure completeness too.

10
Lexical Resources

David Ogilvy once said, 'If you are both soft and sentimental, you are in the wrong business. I would like to meet a poet who is a killer.' This quote underscores Ogilvy's belief that effective copywriting requires a balance between creativity and a results-oriented, persuasive approach.

In the context of choosing appropriate lexical resources, Ogilvy's concept of combining the roles of poet and killer is particularly relevant. This dual nature emphasises the need to balance artistic expression with a clear, compelling message. For instance, when editing AI-generated content, it is crucial to blend creative flair with precise, persuasive language. The poet's finesse ensures the content is engaging and resonates emotionally with the audience, while the killer's precision guarantees that the message is direct, persuasive, and aligned with the brand's objectives. By incorporating this balanced approach, content creators can craft messages that are both captivating and effective.

When editing for appropriate lexical resources, it is important to carefully consider the audience's language preferences, industry-specific terminologies, and the overall tone that resonates with them. Just as a poet carefully selects words to evoke emotions, the language used in AI-generated content must resonate with the audience and prompt the intended response. At the same time, a killer's instinct calls for clarity and precision, ensuring there is no ambiguity, miscommunication, or potential disconnect.

To make AI-generated content as efficacious as possible, content writers need to navigate through the content with the acumen of a seasoned copywriter (even if the content is an article or an email). They must ensure that the lexical resources employed not only showcase the creative flair essential for engagement but also align with the strategic objectives of the brand. This nuanced editing process ensures that AI-generated content not only captures attention but also persuades and resonates, much like the timeless wisdom imparted by David Ogilvy.

In the following section, we will explore key aspects of lexical resources that require careful attention when editing generative AI content.

Lexical Essentials: Critical Focus Areas in AI Content Editing

In the rapidly evolving landscape of AI-generated content, understanding the nuances of language is crucial. Let's explore the key linguistic elements that form the foundation of well-crafted content, guiding you through the essential aspects of language that can make or break the quality and impact of your work.

1. Diversity of Vocabulary

Understanding the 'diversity of vocabulary' in editing generative AI responses involves a nuanced approach to the words and expressions that shape the content. Think of language as a symphony, where each word plays a unique role in creating the overall harmony. Our editorial focus, therefore, should be on crafting a composition that is both rich and varied.

In practical terms, this means avoiding the monotony of repetition, which can dull the impact of the content. Just as a persistent drumbeat can lose its effect, repetitive language can weaken the message. Instead, our task is to introduce a kaleidoscope of vocabulary, with each word adding its own distinct colour to the narrative. Hence, editors should strive for a harmonious blend of synonyms, antonyms, and varied phrasing. Like a painter selecting the perfect palette to evoke emotion, we must choose words that not only convey the intended meaning but also evoke a deeper response from the reader. For example, if the AI-generated content relies heavily on a particular term, the editor's role is to identify opportunities for lexical expansion. This might involve introducing synonyms, exploring alternative expressions, or selecting words with subtle differences in meaning. The goal is to elevate the content from a repetitive monotone to a rich symphony of linguistic diversity. Additionally, the skill of editing here involves crafting language that is not only informative but also visually appealing, ensuring that the depth of vocabulary resonates with the audience in a memorable and impactful way.

All in all, by integrating this variety into the structure of the content, content creators and editors can enhance the reading experience.

2. Appropriateness of Terminology

Conversely, in a more casual or colloquial setting, appropriateness pivots towards embracing a language that aligns with the informality of the context and involves selecting expressions that resonate with the intended audience, creating a conversational cadence that feels natural and relatable. Editors, in this role, act as linguistic architects, ensuring that the edifice of terminology stands sturdy and congruent. It involves meticulous attention to detail, a discerning eye to spot incongruities, and a nuanced understanding of the intended audience and purpose.

In practice, this editing principle encourages a dynamic engagement with the content. It prompts us to question whether the language used is the most fitting and effective means of communication within the given parameters. A judicious selection of terminology not only enhances clarity but also contributes to the overall persuasiveness and impact of the AI-generated response.

Ultimately, appropriateness of terminology isn't just a linguistic checkbox; it is a deliberate and thoughtful crafting of language that ensures the AI response resonates harmoniously within its designated context.

3. Avoidance of Ambiguity

Understanding and implementing the principles of 'avoidance of Ambiguity' in the editing process is like ensuring a clear path for readers. This guarantees that as readers engage with the content, they experience clarity and comprehension. This editing principle underscores the significance of crystal-clear communication, urging the editor to dispel any fog of ambiguity that might obscure the meaning.

The scrutiny of the editors should extend to every nook and cranny of the response, checking for language that might be open to multiple interpretations or could leave the reader pondering the intended meaning. They need to craft a narrative where each word serves as a precise marker, leaving no room for misdirection.

The avoidance of ambiguity also hinges on the nuanced selection of lexical resources. It prompts us to assess whether the words chosen are not only accurate in conveying the intended message but also devoid of multiple meanings that could sow seeds of confusion. Precision becomes the editorial compass, guiding us to select words and phrases that leave no room for misinterpretation.

In practical terms, this editing principle encourages a meticulous examination of phrases, sentences, and expressions that might be construed in different ways. This, in turn, fosters a narrative where each word contributes unequivocally to the overall meaning, allowing the reader to traverse the content with confidence and comprehension. Moreover, clarity in lexical choices not only aids understanding but elevates the overall quality of the AI-generated content. It transforms the content from a potential labyrinth of uncertainty into a well-lit, navigable path, enhancing the reader's experience and reinforcing the credibility of the generated response.

4. Consistency in Tone

Imagine the AI-generated response as a narrative with its own tonal nuances, akin to the different instruments in an orchestra. As editors, we need to guide the lexical choices to ensure a consistent tonal melody, avoiding discordant notes that could disrupt the reader's experience.

Consistency in tone isn't just about repeating the same words; it is about creating a linguistic atmosphere that matches the mood and purpose of the content. Whether the tone is formal, conversational, informative, or persuasive, our goal is to ensure that every word contributes to a harmonious flow.

Lexical choices serve as the palette for painting the tonal landscape. Each word, like a brushstroke, shapes the overall tone, and our editorial oversight ensures that these strokes blend seamlessly. This consistency in word choice not only enhances readability but also strengthens the coherence of the message, preventing any jarring shifts that might distract or confuse the reader.

In practical terms, our editorial ear is attuned to the tonal nuances that echo through the content. Content writers and editors need to scrutinise each word, asking whether it resonates with the established tone and contributes to the overall ambience. Simply put, it is about crafting a narrative where the tone is a steady undercurrent, providing a cohesive reading experience from the opening sentence to the final punctuation mark.

Ultimately, maintaining consistency in tone through strategic lexical choices is about creating a literary composition that sings in unison. It ensures that the reader, much like an audience, can immerse themselves in the content without being disrupted by discordant notes, fostering engagement and understanding.

5. Cultural Sensitivity

It is crucial to consider cultural nuances and sensitivities when selecting words. Lexical choices should reflect cultural norms and avoid language that could be perceived as offensive or inappropriate. Editors must navigate these nuances carefully, ensuring that their word choices not only communicate the intended message but also respect and align with diverse cultural contexts.

Think of language as a bridge between different cultures. Every word has the power to either build connections or create divides. As editors, our goal is to foster inclusivity and understanding by choosing words that respect cultural sensitivities and enhance the overall harmony of the content. Moreover, cultural sensitivity extends beyond avoiding blatant pitfalls; it involves a nuanced dance with lexical choices that reflect an awareness of cultural contexts. Meaning, it is about selecting words that resonate positively, acknowledging the diverse perspectives and sensitivities that readers bring to the content. Our editorial lens becomes a filter, sieving out any potential linguistic missteps that might inadvertently cause discomfort or offence. Practically, this involves a meticulous examination of words, phrases, and idioms to ensure they align with the cultural norms relevant to the content.

In essence, incorporating cultural sensitivity into lexical resources is an exercise in empathy. It is about recognising that words carry weight beyond their literal meanings and, as writers and editors, taking responsibility for the impact these words may have. Through this conscientious approach, we contribute to a more inclusive, respectful, and globally accessible narrative.

In conclusion, balancing lexical resources is key in refining AI-generated content to improve its quality, clarity, and overall impact.

Key Takeaways

1. Make sure that the content has effective lexical resources.
2. Ensure that the lexical resources employed are consistent with the overall tone of the content.
3. Ensure that the vocabulary used is culturally sensitive and aligns with industry standards.

11
Coherence and Cohesion

Seth Godin, a renowned marketing expert, famously advised, 'Be remarkable.' This advice is crucial for standing out in today's digital information overload. Godin's call to be remarkable emphasises that your content should shine amid the vast sea of information. And in the quest for remarkability, coherence plays a vital role. It acts as the binding thread, connecting ideas logically and creating a captivating narrative. Additionally, coherence ensures that your content flows naturally, guiding readers through a logical progression that's both informative and engaging.

An important point to note here is that a remarkable piece of content grabs attention from the start, delivers its message smoothly, and leaves a lasting impression. Coherence ensures that every part of your content works harmoniously, making the overall message clear and compelling. Ultimately, coherence is essential for creating remarkable content. It helps your audience navigate your message with ease and appreciate its value. Whether drawing on Godin's marketing insights or other captivating themes, coherence is an important aspect that will make sure that your content truly stands out.

Benefits of Coherence and Cohesion

The benefits of incorporating coherence and cohesion into your content are manifold, serving as cornerstones for effective communication. Firstly, these elements enhance the overall clarity of your message. A coherent and cohesive piece of content ensures that ideas are logically connected, allowing the audience to follow the narrative effortlessly. With a well-structured flow of ideas, your content becomes more digestible, keeping your audience engaged and preventing confusion or frustration.

Secondly, coherence and cohesion contribute significantly to the readability and user experience of your content. When your ideas are interconnected in a seamless manner, readers can navigate through the information without feeling disjointed. This improved readability not only encourages continued engagement but also fosters a positive impression of your brand or message. Whether it is a blog post, marketing copy, or any other form of content, the benefits of coherence and cohesion extend beyond mere organisation—they create an enjoyable and impactful reading experience. Ultimately, content that exhibits these qualities has the potential to leave a lasting impression, solidifying your brand as a reliable source of information and enhancing your overall communication strategy.

The coherence of AI-generated content depends on various factors, including the quality of the training data, the complexity of the task, and the sophistication of the underlying language model. While AI models have made significant advancements in understanding context and generating coherent text, they may still face challenges in certain scenarios. AI models, such as GPT-3, are trained on vast datasets to understand patterns and generate contextually relevant responses. In many cases, they can produce coherent and contextually appropriate content. However, challenges may arise when generating content on highly specific or nuanced topics where the model may lack domain-specific knowledge.

Additionally, AI-generated content may sometimes lack the creative or intuitive coherence that a human writer might bring to the table. Human writers often inject unique perspectives, emotions, and nuances into their writing that can enhance the overall coherence and depth of the content. Apparently, while AI-generated content can exhibit impressive coherence in many instances, it may not always match the nuanced and creative coherence of human-generated content, especially in specialised or creative fields. Therefore, it is essential to carefully review and, if necessary, edit AI-generated content to ensure it meets the desired level of coherence for a given context.

In the following section, we will explore steps you can take to achieve coherence and cohesion in your editing process.

Crafting Cohesion: Strategies for a Seamless and Logical Content Structure

Let's examine the key elements essential for creating content that flows smoothly and maintains a logical structure. By focusing on how ideas connect and build upon each other, you will learn effective techniques to ensure that your content not only reads smoothly but also effectively communicates its intended message. This exploration will provide you with practical strategies to enhance the overall readability and unity of your edited work.

1. **Review Overall Structure**

When reviewing the overall structure of generative AI content, our goal as an editor is to ensure that the narrative unfolds in a coherent and organised manner, providing a seamless reading experience. Think of the content as a carefully crafted story, where each element is purposefully positioned to support the overarching narrative.

To achieve this, begin by taking a holistic view of the content, similar to surveying a landscape before building a structure. Assess the arrangement of ideas, concepts, and information to ensure they flow logically from one point to the next. This process is akin to fitting together puzzle pieces, where each component should integrate smoothly into the larger picture without causing confusion. Next, imagine the reader as a traveller navigating your content. The path should be clearly defined, avoiding unexpected detours or abrupt changes. A well-organised structure not only enhances comprehension but also engages the reader, making them more likely to stay interested.

In essence, reviewing the overall structure is about crafting a narrative that is more than just a series of sentences—it is about creating a cohesive and compelling story. This approach serves as the blueprint for ensuring that every element contributes to the content's purpose, resulting in a harmonious and impactful piece that resonates with the reader.

2. Check Transition Words and Phrases

When evaluating transition words and phrases in generative AI content, think of them as the connective tissue that links ideas together, ensuring a seamless and coherent narrative. Transition words are crucial for guiding readers through the content, helping them navigate shifts and relationships between ideas smoothly. Imagine transition words as road signs or guiding lights on a journey. Transition words provide essential cues that prevent readers from getting lost, helping them understand how one idea connects to the next and maintaining a sense of continuity. They indicate changes, show how ideas are related, and ensure a smooth flow.

When assessing transition words, look at their variety and appropriateness. Are they fulfilling their role effectively? Do they clearly indicate contrast, addition, consequence, or progression? Their presence should enhance comprehension and fit the context. Additionally, make sure these linguistic markers are strategically placed to create a logical and well-defined path for the reader.

For example, 'however' indicates a contrast, signalling a change in direction. 'Moreover,' on the other hand, adds additional information, while 'therefore' shows a cause-and-effect relationship. Properly using these transitions ensures that readers can easily follow and understand the content.

In summary, checking transition words and phrases is about refining the structure of your content, ensuring that the journey through your narrative is both intellectually engaging and easy for readers to follow.

3. Evaluate Sentence Structure

When evaluating sentence structure in generative AI content, the goal is to create a smooth, engaging flow that captures and holds the reader's attention. To achieve this, start by considering the rhythm of your sentences. Varying sentence lengths adds dynamism to your writing. Imagine it as composing music, where a mix of short, punchy sentences and longer, flowing ones creates a harmonious rhythm. This variation helps maintain interest and prevents monotony, similar to the way a well-composed piece of music keeps the listener engaged.

In addition to varying sentence length, assess sentence complexity. Balance simple and complex sentences to match the content's complexity. Just as a conductor blends different sections of an orchestra, you are crafting a symphony of sentences that work together seamlessly. This balance ensures clarity while maintaining reader engagement.

Another crucial aspect to consider is the transition between sentences. Just as a seamless segue connects musical movements, sentences should flow smoothly from one to the next, avoiding abrupt shifts that might confuse the reader. To ensure this, assess the logical progression of ideas, making sure each sentence builds on the previous one and contributes to the overall coherence of the text.

In summary, evaluating sentence structure involves crafting a literary composition where each sentence has a distinct role, enhancing the narrative's rhythm, melody, and harmony. This careful process transforms a series of sentences into a cohesive and engaging symphony of words, ensuring clarity and maintaining reader interest.

4. Maintain Consistent Tone

Maintaining a consistent tone in generative AI content is essential for ensuring smooth and coherent communication. Just as a steady rhythm is crucial for the musicality of a conversation, a consistent tone helps keep the narrative flowing seamlessly. Abrupt changes in tone can disrupt the reader's experience, much like sudden shifts in rhythm can jar a listener.

Consistency in tone is achieved through careful lexical choices, which act like musical notes creating a melody. Each word should harmonise with the others to form a unified tone, whether it is formal, conversational, informative, or persuasive. A sudden shift in tone, similar to an unexpected change from a serious to a casual conversation, can confuse the reader and break the coherence of the text.

Choosing the right words is crucial for maintaining tone. Different words evoke different emotions and nuances, and it is important to select ones that align with the desired tone and maintain consistency throughout. For example, in content aiming for a professional and informative tone, using formal and precise language is essential. Introducing informal or colloquial terms can disrupt the intended tone and create dissonance.

In summary, maintaining a consistent tone involves creating a harmonious linguistic melody that resonates with the reader. Each word contributes to the overall tone, ensuring a coherent and engaging reading experience.

5. Use Pronouns and References Wisely

The strategic use of pronouns and references in generative AI content is crucial for guiding readers smoothly through the text. Just as clear road signs help travellers navigate a route, proper pronoun usage and explicit references ensure that readers can follow the narrative without confusion.

Pronouns like he, she, it, and they enhance readability and contribute to the natural flow of sentences. However, their effectiveness depends on clear antecedents—the nouns or phrases they refer to. Without well-defined antecedents, readers may struggle to connect ideas, similar to how ambiguous road signs can hinder navigation.

Similarly, explicit references to previous ideas or concepts act as signposts, helping readers recall and link information. Clear references maintain continuity and prevent disorientation, much like recognisable landmarks guide travellers. For instance, in the sentence, 'The research study yielded significant results. They provide valuable insights into the topic,' the pronoun 'They' clearly points back to 'results,' guiding the reader's understanding.

Effective use of pronouns and references enhances coherence in generative AI content, ensuring a smooth narrative flow and helping readers grasp the connections between ideas. It is about providing clear guidance, fostering understanding, and maintaining engagement throughout the content.

6. Check for Repetition

Repetition, when employed thoughtfully, can reinforce key ideas, similar to a recurring musical motif that strengthens the thematic core. However, excessive repetition is akin to a musical piece with the same notes played repeatedly, dulling the overall impact. Therefore, while editing AI-generated content, it's essential to act as a conductor, carefully orchestrating the use of language. Imagine a melody played on a piano—each note contributes to the overall composition. In the same way, each word in written content plays a specific role. If a note is repeated too often, the melody loses its charm. Similarly, if a word or idea is excessively reiterated, the impact of the message diminishes.

To maintain a harmonious rhythm in content, editors should explore synonyms and varied expressions. Consider this example: 'The project showcased remarkable innovation. The innovation was evident in various aspects of the project.' Here, replacing the second instance of 'innovation' with a synonym or expressing the idea differently would enhance the overall flow and impact.

In essence, addressing repetition in AI-generated content is an artistic endeavour, ensuring that the linguistic melody remains captivating and harmonious. By striking the right balance, editors can compose a narrative that resonates with readers, making the content a compelling and engaging piece.

7. Consider Parallelism

Parallelism in writing is akin to the synchronised movements of a well-choreographed dance—it brings harmony and order to the composition. Just as dancers move in parallel, sentences and lists that exhibit parallel structure contribute to a smooth and cohesive reading experience.

Parallel construction involves maintaining consistency in the structure of phrases, clauses, or items in a list. This not only adds rhythm but also enhances the clarity and flow of the written content. Moreover, parallelism ensures that similar grammatical structures are used for similar ideas. For instance, consider the sentence: 'She likes hiking, swimming, and to ride a bike.' To achieve parallelism, the sentence can be revised as: 'She likes hiking, swimming, and biking.' This adjustment creates a more symmetrical and harmonious structure.

Editors, acting as the choreographers of language, should pay attention to parallelism to maintain a consistent rhythm and ensure that each element in a sentence or list contributes cohesively to the overall composition. Overall, by incorporating parallel construction, editors enhance the readability of the content, allowing readers to follow the graceful flow of ideas and ensuring a captivating literary performance.

8. Create Logical Connections

Crafting a well-structured piece of writing involves creating seamless connections between ideas. Just as a bridge links two shores, effective writing links thoughts and concepts, guiding the reader smoothly through the text.

To ensure clear and intuitive progression, editors must craft transitions between paragraphs and sentences that connect concepts logically. Consider the relationships between cause and effect, comparison and contrast, or chronological events—these elements contribute to a cohesive narrative. Logical connections also keep readers engaged by making the narrative flow naturally and coherently. For example, when discussing technology's impact on communication, smooth transitions between positive and negative aspects prevent abrupt shifts and help readers follow the author's reasoning.

All in all, editors, as architects of clarity, should focus on building these logical connections. By doing so, they facilitate a reader's journey through the narrative, ensuring coherence and a well-structured literary landscape.

9. Consider Reader's Perspective

When editing content, it is essential to adopt the reader's perspective. This approach ensures you align the editing process with the reader's understanding and engagement. From this viewpoint, assess how each sentence and paragraph contributes to the overall clarity and coherence. Consider whether the narrative builds logically on previous concepts and if transitions between ideas are smooth. This perspective helps you craft content that feels intuitive and meets the reader's expectations.

By focusing on the reader's perspective, you enhance both clarity and coherence, shaping a narrative that not only conveys information effectively but also engages the reader. This method goes beyond grammar and syntax, embracing the art of communication to create an immersive experience where the reader is actively involved in the comprehension journey.

In essence, viewing the content through the reader's lens ensures that coherence becomes a reader-centric quality, enhancing the overall impact of the narrative.

10. Seek Feedback

In the collaborative space of content creation, seeking feedback is like opening a window to fresh perspectives. It introduces an invaluable external gaze that can illuminate blind spots and refine the coherence and cohesion of the narrative. This external viewpoint can offer insights that, in the solitary landscape of editing, might have eluded your scrutiny. Others may catch nuances, identify potential gaps, or suggest improvements that contribute to the overall coherence of the content.

Feedback serves as a mirror that reflects not only how well the content aligns with your intended message but also how it resonates with a diverse audience. It is a tool for understanding how the narrative flows in the minds of others, providing a holistic perspective that goes beyond individual subjectivity. Moreover, the act of seeking feedback fosters a collaborative spirit. It transforms the editing process into a shared endeavour, where multiple minds converge to refine and polish the narrative. This collaborative effort not only enhances coherence but also cultivates a sense of ownership among contributors, creating a narrative that is robust, refined, and resonant.

However, it is essential to approach feedback with an open mind, recognising it as a constructive tool for improvement. Different perspectives may lead to varying suggestions, and the art lies in discerning which aligns with the overarching goals of the content.

In summary, seeking feedback is a dynamic step in the editing process that transforms the act of refining coherence and cohesion into a collaborative venture. It is a testament to the recognition that the richness of a narrative often lies in the diversity of perspectives that shape and enhance its overall quality.

To conclude this chapter, mastering the art of editing for coherence and cohesion requires a meticulous orchestration of various elements we have explored. Achieving coherence involves ensuring that each idea flows logically into the next, while cohesion demands that these ideas are seamlessly connected through effective transitions and consistent tone. By carefully balancing these aspects, editors enhance the readability and impact of the content. This approach not only refines the structure but also ensures that the narrative resonates with clarity and engagement, providing a polished and compelling final product.

Key Takeaways

1. Ensure a logical progression of ideas, allowing each element to naturally connect with the next.
2. Maintain a consistent tone throughout, avoiding abrupt shifts that may disrupt the narrative's coherence.

3. Varied sentence structures and lengths contribute to a more dynamic and engaging reading experience.
4. Strive to eliminate unnecessary repetition, opting for diverse expressions and synonyms.
5. Consider the reader's perspective to guarantee that the narrative unfolds logically and progressively.
6. Seek feedback from others to gain valuable insights and refine the narrative collaboratively.

Part III
Customisation

12
Creativity

NEIL PATEL'S JOURNEY FROM A BUDDING ENTREPRENEUR TO a digital marketing expert serves as a compelling anecdote illustrating the profound impact of creativity on content creation. Early in his career, Patel recognised the need for innovation in navigating the intricacies of SEO and online marketing. His exploration of algorithms and strategies reflected not just technical expertise but a creative approach to problem-solving.

As Patel immersed himself in content creation, he recognised that creativity wasn't confined to artistic expression but played a pivotal role in making content more readable and accessible. The landscape of digital marketing demanded not only technical prowess but also the ability to communicate complex concepts in a way that resonated with a broader audience. Creativity became the bridge that connected the technical nuances of SEO with the broader spectrum of online users.

In the field of content marketing, Patel's advice to 'focus on providing value to your audience' underscores the idea that creativity plays a crucial role in making content both engaging and informative. Creative content isn't just about looking good; it is about delivering information in a way that captures and keeps the audience's attention. Patel's own success story demonstrates how creativity can make content more engaging, easier to understand, and more valuable to the reader.

Therefore, we can see how in a world overflowing with information, creativity is the key to cutting through the noise and ensuring that content fulfills its purpose effectively. In this chapter, we will delve into the strategies and techniques that harness creativity to elevate content, making it deeply resonant with the audience.

Key Steps for Ensuring Creative Quality in Content

Creativity, by its nature, eludes a precise scale of measurement, relying more on your intuitive assessment. However, there are specific steps you can take to ensure that the content exhibits an adequate level of creativity. Let's review them.

1. Consider the appropriateness of the language used. In more serious contexts, the tone and style should align with the gravity of the subject matter. Thus, it is crucial to strike a balance where creativity enhances rather than detracts from the overall message.
2. Evaluate the coherence of ideas presented. Creative content should not sacrifice clarity. Ensure that the narrative flows logically and that creative elements enhance rather than obscure the meaning. You have read about it in detail in the previous chapter.

3. Gauge the overall impact of the content. Does it engage the reader? Does it provoke thought or emotion? Creativity, in this context, should contribute to a more compelling and memorable user experience.

In essence, the evaluation of creativity becomes a nuanced task, relying on a blend of your instincts and these strategic considerations to ensure that AI-generated content strikes the right balance between innovation and relevance.

Strategic Creativity: Balancing Type and Audience Needs

When leveraging AI for creative purposes, it is essential to consider two critical aspects: the type of content and the target audience. Understanding the nature of the content—whether it is informational, persuasive, or narrative—guides how creativity should be applied to ensure it aligns with the content's goals. Additionally, tailoring creativity to resonate with the target audience is crucial, as different demographics have varying preferences and expectations. By adjusting creative elements based on these factors, you can enhance the relevance and impact of the content, ensuring it effectively engages and meets the needs of the audience.

1. **Type of Content**

   When editing generative AI content, assessing creativity becomes a crucial rubric, and a determining factor for this evaluation is the type of content being generated. Understanding the nature of your content serves as a compass for calibrating the appropriate level of creativity. For instance, when creating a product manual where clarity and precision are crucial, it is wise to steer clear of literary devices like alliteration, personification, or onomatopoeia, as they might distract from the straightforward information the reader needs. However, it is also important to recognise that even within the rigid structure of a manual, there's room for creativity.

Let's look at the following example where AI-driven creativity has transformed the table of contents, making it more aligned with modern preferences rather than sticking to a purely procedural format.

Traditional Manual	**AI-Generated Creative Content**
1. Introduction	1. Quick Start Guide
1.1. Overview of Mixer Grinder	1.1. Get to Know Your Mixer Grinder
1.2. Purpose and Scope of the Manual	1.2. Simple Setup for First-time Users
2. Safety Precautions	2. Safety Made Easy
2.1. General Safety Guidelines	2.1. Handy Safety Tips
2.2. Handling Tips	2.2. Hasle-free Handling
3. Unpacking and Assembly	3. Easy Assembly
3.1. Parts and Components Overview	3.1. Visual Guide for Components
3.2. Assembling the Mixer Grinder	3.2. Snap and Pay: How to Assemble
4. Operating Instructions	4. Effortless Operation
4.1. Powering On/Off	4.1. One, Two, and Go: On/Off
4.2. Correct Usage Strategies	4.2. Mixer Mastery: Best Practices
5. Cleaning and Maintenance	5. Easy Cleanup and Maintenance
5.1. Cleaning Practices	5.1. Speedy Cleanup
5.2. Maintenance Practices	5.2. Maintenance Made Manageable
5.3. Troubleshooting Common Issues	5.3. DIY Fixes for Common Issues
6. Warranty and Support	6. Warranty and Support
6.1. Warranty Information	6.1. Warranty Details
6.2. Customer Support	6.2. Get Help Fast

Thus, we can see how a creative approach can not only make content more appealing but also simplify complex concepts, presenting information in a way that enhances user comprehension.

When working with non-fiction content, creativity plays a unique yet crucial role. The primary objective of such content is to engage the reader while simplifying complex issues. AI-generated responses should reflect this approach, ensuring that the content is both accessible and informative. Conversely, in fiction, creativity acts as the foundation of storytelling, where the deliberate crafting of plot, character development, and thematic depth results in a cohesive and captivating narrative. The key takeaway here is that creativity in generative AI responses should enhance the overall structure, coherence, and clarity of the content. It is not merely about adding creative elements but using creativity as a tool to improve comprehension and user experience.

Let's look at a short story I wrote, featuring vampires, witches, and werewolves, in a narrative format.

In the mystical city of Kerelyn, where magical beings coexisted harmoniously, a dark secret lurked beneath the veneer of unity. Nightraven, the venerable vampire king, ruled with an iron fist, his regal demeanour concealing a malevolent force. The city's enchantment began to unravel when a witch, Rowena, was found dead under mysterious circumstances.

A private investigator among the witches, Seraphina, delved into the shadows to uncover the truth. What she discovered sent shivers down her spine. King Nightraven had been harbouring a nefarious secret, one that shattered the illusion of harmony among the magical beings. Deep beneath the sprawling city, dungeons echoed with the anguished cries of witches and werewolves, once revered and now prisoners of the vampire king's tyranny.

The captives lived in compromised circumstances, their magic dampened, and their spirits broken. Seraphina, driven by a sense of justice, rallied her fellow witches and formed an alliance with the werewolves. Together, they embarked on a perilous journey to expose the malevolence that tainted the once-glorious city.

As whispers of rebellion spread through Kerelyn, the alliance faced challenges from all corners. Nightraven, sensing the imminent threat to his reign, unleashed his dark magic upon them. The witches and werewolves, however, were fueled by a collective desire for freedom and justice.

The final confrontation unfolded beneath the ancient oak tree in the heart of Kerelyn. Spells clashed, claws clashed, and the city's fate hung in the balance. Seraphina, wielding the power of her coven, confronted Nightraven in a battle that resonated with the echoes of centuries-old grievances.

In the end, justice prevailed. The vampire king was vanquished, and the witches and werewolves were liberated from their subterranean prison. The city of Kerelyn, now purged of its malevolent ruler, began the arduous journey of rebuilding and rediscovering the true essence of magical coexistence. The tale of Nightraven and the rebellion became a cautionary legend, a reminder that even in the realm of magic, tyranny could be overthrown by the strength of unity and the pursuit of justice.

Now let's examine the same story with enhancements made through AI-driven creativity.

In the bewitched realm of Kerelyn, where mystical beings danced in moonlit harmony, a shadow concealed a chilling secret. Nightraven, the regal vampire king, draped in darkness, ruled with an unseen malevolence. The enchantment that cloaked the city began to fray when the lifeless body of Rowena, a once-celebrated witch, was discovered under a shroud of mystery.

Seraphina, a witch endowed with an inquisitive spirit, embarked on a clandestine journey into the ethereal underbelly of Kerelyn. Her pursuit of the truth unfurled a tapestry of horror—King Nightraven had woven a web of deceit. Deep beneath the city, forgotten dungeons echoed with the lamentations of witches and werewolves, once revered, now captive to the vampiric sovereign's tyranny.

In the dim-lit confines of their subterranean prisons, magic waned, and spirits withered. Seraphina, guided by the flames of justice, gathered her kin, and a pact was forged with the forgotten werewolves. Together, an alliance against the tyranny of Nightraven was born, destined to expose the underbelly of Kerelyn's once-glorious facade.

As whispers of rebellion coalesced with the night wind, challenges emerged. Nightraven, sensing the impending upheaval, unleashed dark magic upon the dissenters. The air crackled with enchantments as the fate of Kerelyn teetered on the precipice. The oak tree, ancient and wise, bore witness to the climax of this ethereal drama.

In the epic confrontation, the clash of spells and the fury of claws painted the canvas of Kerelyn's destiny. Seraphina, a beacon of the coven's power, faced Nightraven in a showdown that resonated with the echoes of age-old grievances.

Justice, embodied by the alliance of witches and werewolves, triumphed. Nightraven's dark reign crumbled, and the prisoners of Kerelyn's abyss emerged into the moonlit freedom. The city, cleansed of malevolence, embraced the dawn of renewal, as the tapestry of magic was rewoven, illustrating the resilience of unity, the strength of justice, and the eternal dance of mystical coexistence.

In conclusion, the nature of the content should act as a guiding principle, directing how creativity is applied to meet its specific objectives. By aligning creative efforts with the content's goals, we ensure that each element—be it the structure, tone, or style—serves a purpose and contributes to achieving the desired impact. This alignment helps in crafting content that not only captivates the audience but also fulfils its intended purpose with precision.

2. Target Audience

Understanding your target audience is a pivotal factor in shaping the creativity of your content. Consider who your readers are—are they corporate managers operating from highly tech-savvy boardrooms, or are they individuals seeking insights from the comfort of their homes? Tailoring the creative elements of the content is contingent upon the characteristics and expectations of your intended audience.

The aspect of tailoring content to specific target groups (TG) is becoming all the more important in today's world dominated by consumer goods and products. Understanding this helps in selecting the right lexical resources that resonate with your audience. Let's illustrate this with a real-life example:

Consider air conditioners, a common household item. The factors influencing a person's choice of air conditioner can vary widely based on their individual needs and preferences. Consider, for example, my husband, a Ph.D. in optical fibre communications, who evaluates products based on technical specifications and prefers brands that meet his engineering standards. In contrast, my approach to purchasing items focuses on sleek design and ease of use. This difference in preferences was evident when choosing a new mobile phone: I prioritised colour and camera features, while he emphasised the importance of the operating system (OS).

Returning to product descriptions, it is evident that the readership generally falls into two categories: technical and non-technical. Each group requires a tailored approach to effectively address their preferences and needs. For a tech-savvy audience, the description should focus on detailed technical specifications and features. Conversely, for a non-technical audience, simplicity is key. Using clear language and relatable metaphors helps make complex technical details more accessible and engaging. This approach ensures that the product is presented in a way that resonates with each segment of the audience.

Based on these observations, I have created two distinct product descriptions for an air conditioner, each tailored to a specific audience: one for a technical audience and one for a non-technical audience. Review these examples closely to identify the differences in tone and structure between the two descriptions.

Product Description for a Technical Audience

Introducing the XYZ 2-Ton Air Conditioner—a marvel of cooling technology engineered for enthusiasts seeking superior performance. This advanced cooling unit boasts an innovative inverter technology that adapts to your cooling needs, providing precise temperature control without compromising energy efficiency. Equipped with R-32 refrigerant, it not only cools effectively but also minimises environmental impact, ensuring sustainability. The intelligent air swing feature ensures uniform cooling throughout the room, while the advanced filters keep the air pure and allergen-free. With a user-friendly interface and smart connectivity options, this XYZ AC puts you in control, offering an unmatched cooling experience for the discerning tech enthusiast.

Product Description for a Non-technical Audience

Experience comfort without compromise with the XYZ 2-Ton Air Conditioner—designed for those who seek efficient cooling with a keen eye on energy savings. This eco-friendly cooling solution features a high Energy Efficiency Ratio (EER), ensuring optimal cooling performance while minimising electricity consumption. The advanced compressor technology delivers powerful cooling while maintaining whisper-quiet operation, making it ideal for both residential and commercial spaces. With intelligent temperature sensors and programmable modes, you can personalise your comfort while optimising energy usage. The XYZ 2-Ton AC is not just about cooling; it's about cooling smartly, providing you with the perfect blend of comfort and energy savings, ensuring a pleasant environment without breaking the bank.

In essence, the target audience serves as a compass, guiding the degree of creativity in your content. Put simply, it is about speaking the language of your readers, whether it is the language of everyday experiences or the nuanced vocabulary of a specific industry. By aligning with your audience's expectations and knowledge levels, you can strike the right balance to make your content both accessible and impactful.

Key Takeaways

1. Creativity is flexible and varies based on the type of content and the intended audience.
2. In non-fiction content, creativity is expressed by simplifying information into easily understandable segments.
3. Creativity is a key component in crafting effective sales pitches and engaging content.

13
Relatability

Seth Godin emphasises that effective content goes beyond the superficial to genuinely connect with your audience. He often highlights the power of storytelling, noting how a compelling narrative has the potential to forge a strong connection with your audience. For example, Godin has discussed how brands which share their journey or the stories of the people behind them build a deeper bond with consumers.

Godin believes that relatability stems from understanding your audience's desires, fears, and aspirations. Addressing these elements allows you to create content that resonates both emotionally and intellectually. For instance, a blog post that not only details a product's features but also includes real customer stories about its impact can add significant depth.

In essence, Godin's advice centres on moving beyond surface-level content to create something truly meaningful and relatable, which helps build a stronger connection with your audience and fosters trust and loyalty.

When it comes to generative AI, it can content that is coherent and contextually relevant based on the input it receives. However, creating content with deep emotional resonance and nuanced understanding often requires a human touch. While AI can generate information and structured text, it might not fully capture the emotional and contextual depth that engages a human audience.

To enhance the relatability and impact of AI-generated content, it is essential to review and refine it critically. This might involve adding specific details, anecdotes, or examples to better connect with your target audience. All in all, though AI is a valuable tool in content creation, human oversight and refinement are crucial to achieving the desired level of emotional depth and engagement.

In this chapter, we will explore strategies to enhance the relatability of your content and delve into best practices for optimising it. Additionally, we will discuss how to refine your approach to make your content more engaging and impactful, ultimately leading to a more meaningful interaction with your readers.

Steps to Achieve Content Reliability

Achieving reliability in content generated by AI involves a thoughtful approach and careful refinement. Here is a practical plan to enhance the relatability of your AI-generated content:

1. **Define Your Audience and Purpose**

   To create reliable content, start by clearly defining your target audience and the purpose of your content. Identify who your readers are, including their demographics, interests, and pain points. Understanding these factors helps tailor your content to meet their specific needs and preferences. For example, if your audience consists of busy professionals, you might focus on concise, actionable advice that fits into their hectic schedules. Conversely, for a more academic audience, you might include detailed analyses and references. Knowing your audience helps ensure that the content is relevant and engaging.

2. **Craft a Detailed Prompt**

Provide a detailed and specific prompt to the AI, outlining the key points, emotions, and context you want the content to cover. The more information you provide, the better the AI can understand your expectations. Let's look at an example to understand this better.

Vague Prompt: Write a blog article about overcoming work-related stress.

Detailed Prompt: I found out that my readers often face deep stress at the workplace. Write a stepwise action plan in the form of a blog article to help them overcome this stress. Write at least 1200 words in friendly conversational tones including examples.

3. **Engage in Multiple Iterations**

Creating effective content often requires several rounds of refinement. Engage in multiple iterations by generating initial drafts, reviewing them for relevance and clarity, and refining them as needed. Each iteration allows you to adjust the tone, improve coherence, and ensure the content better meets your audience's needs. For example, after receiving an initial draft from the AI, you might identify areas where the content lacks depth or clarity and revise those sections accordingly. This iterative process helps in fine-tuning the content to achieve a higher level of reliability and engagement.

4. **Evaluate Impactful Statements**

Identify and assess key statements or insights within the content that are particularly impactful. Consider how these statements contribute to the overall relatability and effectiveness of the content. For example, if a statement effectively addresses a common concern or provides a powerful solution, highlight it to ensure it stands out. Evaluating these impactful statements helps ensure that your content resonates with your audience and leaves a lasting impression.

5. **Check for Diverse Perspectives**

Incorporating diverse perspectives can enrich your content and make it more relatable to a wider audience. Aim to present multiple viewpoints on the topic to provide a comprehensive understanding. For instance, if you're writing about a controversial issue, include different sides of the argument to offer a balanced discussion. This approach helps engage readers who may have varying opinions or experiences, making the content more inclusive and relatable.

6. **Add a Personal Touch and Anecdotes**

Infuse the content with personal anecdotes, real-life examples, or relatable stories that add a human touch.

This helps in creating a connection with the audience and adds depth to the narrative. However, it is important to note that the type of content will ultimately determine whether personal anecdotes or factual information from other sources should be used. For instance, when writing about climate change, personal experiences can add valuable perspective. Conversely, for a topic like juvenile crime, it is more suitable to cite reliable sources such as newspapers and videos to ensure factual accuracy.

7. Incorporate Emotional Appeal

Introduce elements of emotion and empathy for increasing engagement and level of connection. Consider how the content will resonate emotionally with your audience and accordingly, share experiences that evoke emotions and make the content more memorable. The step aligns with the principles of David Ogilvy, often considered the father of advertising. While not explicitly stating emotions driving actions, Ogilvy asserts the persuasive power of emotions in marketing. He believed that successful advertising triggers emotions, influencing people's decisions and actions.

8. Refine and Expand

Identify areas where the content can be expanded or refined. Look for opportunities to explore specific topics more deeply, offering additional insights, explanations, or alternative perspectives. However, it is crucial to navigate the balance between refinement and expansion within standard content size norms. Overly lengthy content might deter readers, causing them to leave the webpage or video. Additionally, considering the nature of different platforms is imperative. Email communications and Instagram captions, for instance, benefit from conciseness, while LinkedIn thrives on data-driven, in-depth content with supporting ideas. The approach, of course, hinges on the content type and its intended purpose.

9. **Assess Clarity and Engagement**

Ensure that your content is clear and engaging. Use language that enhances readability and keeps the audience's attention. For example, break down complex ideas into simple, digestible segments and use engaging visuals or examples to illustrate key points. Evaluate how well the content captures and holds the reader's interest, and make adjustments to improve clarity and engagement where necessary.

10. **Review AI-Generated Content**

After generating AI content, thoroughly review it for accuracy, coherence, and alignment with your audience's expectations. Check for consistency in tone, clarity of message, and relevance to the intended audience. For instance, if the content is for a professional audience, ensure that it maintains a formal tone and provides valuable insights. A detailed review helps ensure that the final content meets the desired standards and resonates effectively with readers.

11. Continuous Improvement

Treat content creation as an ongoing process of improvement. Analyse the performance of your content, learn from user interactions, and continuously refine your approach to achieve greater relatability and reach over time. By combining the capabilities of generative AI with human insight, creativity, and iterative refinement, you can craft content that not only meets your audience's expectations but also establishes a meaningful connection with them.

By methodically following this plan, you can effectively increase the relatability factor of the AI-generated content while also aligning it with your standards for thoroughness, clarity, and impact.

Key Takeaways

1. Thoroughly review AI-generated content to ensure it includes supporting explanations and relevant examples.
2. Add a personal touch to foster an emotional connection with the reader.
3. Utilise multiple iterations to deepen the content and enhance its value for your audience.

14
Formatting and Style

We have already discussed how Neil Patel, a renowned digital marketing expert and entrepreneur, emphasises the importance of creativity in content. Another key aspect Patel highlights is the significance of formatting. He frequently underscores the importance of user experience and readability in online content, advocating for proper formatting as a crucial factor in engaging and retaining audiences.

Seth Godin echoes this sentiment, stating the importance of clarity and brevity in communication. His philosophy aligns with the idea that well-formatted content—featuring clear headings and an organised structure—resonates more effectively with audiences. He advises marketers to avoid unnecessary complexity and to present information in a format that meets the preferences of their target audience.

Thus, we can see that formatting plays a pivotal role in capturing and maintaining reader attention. It transforms dense, overwhelming text into a more digestible and visually appealing format, making the content more accessible and engaging. By adhering to formatting principles advocated by experts like Neil Patel and Seth Godin, you can enhance the chances of your content achieving maximum readability and impact.

In this chapter, we will explore common formatting challenges when working with AI-generated content and discuss strategies for addressing them to enhance the overall quality and impact of the content.

Formatting Challenges: Identifying Common Issues in AI Content

In the online landscape, where attention spans are short and users often skim rather than read in detail, effective formatting is crucial. Headings, subheadings, bullet points, and concise paragraphs improve readability, enabling readers to quickly absorb key points and engage more deeply with the content. While generative AI can produce content and even apply some formatting, its results may not always meet your specific preferences or the high standards of experienced marketers. AI typically follows general patterns and structures but lacks the nuanced understanding that a human editor brings to the table.

Let's examine some common formatting inconsistencies in AI-generated content, which can create challenges in achieving a polished and cohesive final product.

1. **Inconsistent Bullet Styles**

   Error: Generative AI may switch between round bullets, square bullets, or numbered lists inconsistently within the text.

   Impact: It can disrupt visual harmony and coherence.

Rectification: Standardise bullet styles throughout the document. Choose a consistent format for lists and adhere to it.

2. **Misaligned Headings**

   Error: Headings and subheadings may be inconsistently formatted in terms of font size, boldness, or alignment.

   Impact: It disrupts the hierarchy and can make the text appear disjointed.

   Rectification: Ensure uniformity in heading formatting. Set a standard for font size, style, and alignment for each level of heading.

3. **Incoherent Font Styles**

   Error: Generative AI might introduce different font styles (bold, italic, underlined) without a clear pattern or purpose.

   Impact: It can distract readers and diminish readability.

   Rectification: Establish guidelines for the use of font styles. Use bold for emphasis and italics for titles and apply these formatting choices consistently throughout the content.

4. **Paragraph Spacing Variations**

   Error: Inconsistent spacing between paragraphs can create a visually cluttered or disjointed appearance.

Impact: It affects readability and the overall flow of the content.

Rectification: Set a standard for paragraph spacing and ensure uniformity throughout the document.

In summary, while generative AI can provide a solid starting point for content creation, it requires refinement through editorial expertise. AI can assist in generating content, but the human touch is essential for ensuring that the content is well-written and effectively formatted for maximum impact.

Best Practices for Effective Formatting

To ensure effective formatting, it is important to follow established best practices that optimise both the layout and functionality of your content. Adhering to these guidelines will enhance readability and engagement, resulting in more impactful content.

1. **Create a Style Guide**

   Establish a style guide that dictates the preferred formatting for headings, lists, fonts, and spacing. This serves as a reference for maintaining consistency.

2. **Manually Review and Edit**

   Carefully review the generative AI response and manually edit formatting errors. Ensure uniformity in elements like bullet points, headings, and fonts.

3. Utilise Text Editing Tools

Leverage text editing tools that allow for bulk formatting adjustments. Use find and replace functions to standardise formatting elements across the document.

4. Preview and Adjust

Preview the document in different formats to identify how formatting appears in various settings. Adjust as needed to ensure consistency in different viewing environments.

5. Iterative Editing

Edit the content iteratively, focusing on specific formatting elements during each pass. This ensures a thorough review and correction of all formatting inconsistencies.

By addressing these common formatting errors systematically, editors can enhance the visual appeal and professionalism of generative AI content, resulting in a publish-ready document with consistent and coherent formatting.

Key Takeaways

1. Check if the H1s and subheadings are correctly written.
2. Review thoroughly to ensure the content flows smoothly and aligns with the intended format.
3. Ensure all the bullet points are consistent.

15
Readability

READABILITY IS A CRITICAL ASPECT OF CONTENT CREATION, and many prominent marketers emphasise its importance. One such figure is Ann Handley, a renowned digital marketing expert and best-selling author. Ann Handley is the chief content officer of MarketingProfs and has shared valuable insights on content marketing.

Ann Handley stresses the importance of creating content that is not only useful and valuable but also readable. In her book "Everybody Writes," she discusses the significance of clear and accessible writing. Handley advocates for simplicity and readability in content to ensure that the audience can easily consume and understand the message being conveyed.

The idea echoed by Ann Handley aligns with the broader consensus in the marketing industry that readability plays a crucial role in engaging and retaining the audience. Crafting content with readability in mind enhances the overall user experience and contributes to the success of content marketing efforts.

In this chapter, we will explore the concept of readability, its importance, the challenges AI-generated content faces in achieving readability, and practical tips for improving it.

Why Readability Matters?

Several factors affect content readability, but generally, content with good readability is well-crafted and easy to read, which increases the likelihood of achieving its intended goals. High readability also enhances the overall effectiveness of the content, making it more impactful and memorable for the audience.

In content editing, readability is crucial due to several factors. Let's examine the key factors that make readability essential in today's content landscape.

1. **User Engagement**

   Readable content enhances user engagement by offering a smooth and enjoyable reading experience. As a result, readers are more inclined to interact with, share, and return to content that is easy to understand.

2. **Attention Spans**

   In today's fast-paced digital environment, readers often have limited attention spans. Therefore, content that is easily readable is more likely to capture and retain the reader's attention.

3. **Cognitive Load**

   Complex and convoluted content may overwhelm readers, leading to disengagement. Readability reduces the cognitive load on readers, allowing them to comprehend and retain information more effectively.

4. **Psychological Impact**

Readability affects how content impacts readers psychologically. Clear, concise, and well-structured content is viewed as more trustworthy and credible.

5. **Accessibility and Inclusivity**

Readable content ensures accessibility for a diverse audience with varying literacy levels. It promotes inclusivity by making information available and understandable to a broader readership.

6. **Content Overload**

In the digital age, readers are inundated with an abundance of content. Readability becomes a distinguishing factor, helping content stand out in the sea of information.

7. **Mobile Consumption**

With the rise of mobile devices, a significant portion of content is consumed on smaller screens. Readable content is essential for a positive mobile user experience.

8. **SEO Impact**

Search engines consider readability when ranking content. Well-structured and readable content is more likely to rank higher, increasing its visibility.

9. **Brand Perception**

Readable content contributes to a positive brand perception. Brands that prioritise clear communication are viewed favourably by audiences.

10. **Behavioural Economics**

Readable content aligns with principles of behavioural economics by catering to cognitive preferences and addressing common cognitive biases.

In conclusion, prioritising readability in content editing recognises the changing dynamics of digital communication. In an information-saturated landscape, making content easily digestible, engaging, and accessible is essential for effectively conveying messages and achieving communication goals.

Readability Challenges in AI Content: Common Issues and Solutions

Generative AI, despite its capabilities, can occasionally produce content with readability issues that may alienate readers who favour clear, concise, and easily digestible information. These issues can range from overly complex sentence structures to inconsistent formatting, potentially impacting the reader's engagement and understanding. Let's examine some of the common readability challenges in AI-generated content.

1. **Inconsistent Tone:** Generative AI can sometimes produce content with abrupt tone shifts, which can be confusing for readers. Consistent tone is essential

for maintaining readability and ensuring a smooth reading experience.

2. **Complex Sentence Structure:** AI may create overly complex sentences that hinder comprehension. Simplifying these structures is often necessary.
3. **Jargon Overuse:** Excessive use of industry jargon can make content difficult for a broader audience to understand.
4. **Lack of Coherence:** Responses may lack logical flow and coherence, jumping between ideas without proper transitions.
5. **Poor Paragraph Structure:** Large, dense paragraphs can be visually overwhelming. Breaking content into smaller paragraphs enhances readability.
6. **Ambiguity and Vagueness:** Ambiguous or vague phrases can lead to unclear messages. Precision in language is crucial.
7. **Inconsistent Formatting:** Errors like inconsistent use of bullets or numbering can disrupt visual flow.
8. **Overuse of Passive Voice:** Excessive passive voice can make sentences convoluted. Editing for clarity often involves converting passive constructions to active voice.
9. **Wordiness and Redundancy:** Verbose content with unnecessary words and redundancy can be streamlined for conciseness.
10. **Lack of Transitional Phrases:** The absence of transitions can result in a choppy narrative. Adding appropriate transitions improves flow.

11. **Overly Formal or Informal Language:** Misjudging the appropriate level of formality for the audience can impact readability.
12. **Ignoring Readability Indices:** The AI may not optimise content based on readability tools like Flesch-Kincaid or Gunning Fog.
13. **Inconsistent Language Complexity:** Language complexity may not consistently match the target audience, leading to readability issues.
14. **Ignoring Cultural Nuances:** Lack of consideration for cultural nuances can make content less relatable to diverse audiences.
15. **Ignoring Readability Tools:** AI may not always use readability tools, potentially missing opportunities for improvements that these tools can identify.

In summary, content writers and editors should ensure that AI-generated material is tailored to the readability preferences of their target audience. By identifying and addressing common readability issues, editors can refine the content, ensuring it is clear and engaging, and ultimately providing a better reading experience.

Mastering Readability: Steps to Refine AI Content

Editing a generative AI response for readability requires a careful balance of assessing quantitative metrics and qualitative aspects. Here are steps to ensure your content not only scores high on readability indices but also resonates with your audience:

1. **Use Readability Tools as a Starting Point**
    - Leverage tools like Flesch-Kincaid for a quantitative analysis of readability.
    - Understand insights on sentence length, word complexity, and overall readability.
    - These tools provide a foundational assessment to guide your editing process.
2. **Consider Target Audience**
    - Tailor your content's readability to match the audience's knowledge level and preferences.
    - Adjust language complexity and sentence structure to align with their expectations.
    - Ensuring the content is accessible enhances engagement.
3. **Assess Sentence and Paragraph Length**
    - Aim for a rhythmic blend of short and long sentences.
    - Break down lengthy paragraphs into smaller, digestible chunks.
    - This balance enhances the natural flow and readability of the content.
4. **Eliminate Unnecessary Complexity**
    - Simplify technical terms and jargon, ensuring clarity for a broader audience.
    - Avoid unnecessary complexity that might hinder comprehension.

- Striking this balance is vital for reader engagement.

5. **Ensure Consistent Tone**
    - Maintain a uniform tone throughout the response to establish a cohesive narrative.
    - Sudden shifts can disrupt the flow and confuse readers, impacting comprehension.
    - Consistency contributes significantly to overall readability.

6. **Check for Coherence and Logical Flow**
    - Review the content to ensure a logical progression of ideas.
    - Smooth transitions between paragraphs contribute to overall coherence.
    - A well-structured narrative enhances the reading experience.

7. **Use Formatting for Clarity**
    - Employ proper formatting with headings, subheadings, and bullet points.
    - Breaking up large blocks of text enhances visual appeal and reader engagement.
    - Visual clarity complements textual coherence.

8. **Read Aloud for Natural Flow**
    - Read the content aloud to identify awkward or stumbling points.
    - Pay attention to the rhythm and natural flow of sentences.

- This practice helps uncover nuances that may be missed during silent reading.

9. **Seek Peer Feedback**
   - Share the content with peers or colleagues for their valuable input.
   - External perspectives can highlight areas that may need improvement.
   - Constructive feedback enriches the editing process.

10. **Address Ambiguities and Redundancies**
    - Clarify any ambiguous statements or sentences that may confuse readers.
    - Remove redundant phrases or information that doesn't contribute to clarity.
    - Precision in language enhances both comprehension and readability.

11. **Consider Contextual Relevance**
    - Ensure that every piece of information aligns with the context and purpose of the content.
    - Avoid unnecessary details that may distract from the main message.
    - Relevance contributes to a focused and reader-friendly narrative.

12. **Use Readability Tools**
    - While readability tools offer valuable insights, prioritise human judgement.

- Ensure the content resonates with your audience beyond what metrics indicate.
- A holistic approach considers both quantitative metrics and qualitative reader experience.

If you incorporate these steps into your editing process, you can enhance the readability of generative AI responses, creating content that not only scores well on readability indices but also captivates and engages your audience effectively.

Key Takeaways

1. Consider both qualitative and quantitative approaches.
2. Readability contributes to positive brand perception.
3. Readable content enhances user engagement.

16

Injecting a Brand Touch

APPLE, A TECH GIANT KNOWN FOR ITS INNOVATION AND sleek design, exemplifies the powerful influence of branding on consumer behaviour. The iconic Apple logo, consistently displayed across its product range, has become synonymous with quality, innovation, and a lifestyle that goes beyond technology.

One of Apple's most significant branding achievements is the immediate recognisability of its logo. The bitten apple represents not just a company, but a culture committed to excellence and cutting-edge technology. The sleek silhouette of an iPhone or the minimalist design of a MacBook instantly evokes the Apple brand, heavily influencing consumer purchasing decisions. Apple also excels in emotional branding, creating a strong connection with consumers by emphasising the experience of using their products rather than just the features. This approach fosters feelings of sophistication, creativity, and belonging to a community that values innovation.

The important takeaway here is that the perceived quality of Apple products reflects the success of its branding strategy.

Consumers view Apple devices not just as functional gadgets, but as status symbols that reflect their taste and lifestyle. This perception drives brand loyalty, encouraging customers to not only upgrade to newer versions but also to become informal brand ambassadors. Apple's integrated ecosystem of devices and services further strengthens this loyalty, creating a reinforcing cycle of continued purchases. In essence, Apple's branding is more than marketing; it is a carefully crafted narrative that resonates deeply with consumers. Apple represents an experience, a lifestyle, and a community, making it not just a tech company, but a cultural phenomenon.

In this chapter, we will explore how to infuse the magic of branding into our writing and elevate our content to the next level.

Key Learnings from Apple's Branding Strategy

Apple's branding strategy offers valuable insights into how a company can transform from a tech provider into a global cultural icon. By examining the core elements of Apple's approach, we can uncover key lessons in building a brand that not only attracts but also deeply resonates with consumers, fostering loyalty and creating a lasting impact on the market.

1. **Emotional Connection Over Features**

   One crucial takeaway from Apple's branding strategy is the emphasis on creating an emotional connection with consumers. Apple doesn't just sell products; it sells an experience, a lifestyle, and a sense of belonging to a community of innovation enthusiasts. When crafting content for a company's products and services, prioritise conveying the experience and emotional impact rather than solely focusing on features. Understand your audience's aspirations and desires, and tailor your content to evoke emotions that align with your brand values.

2. **Consistent Brand Image Across Platforms**

A key factor behind Apple's branding success is its consistent portrayal of the brand image across all platforms. Whether in marketing campaigns, product design, or online presence, Apple maintains a seamless and recognisable brand identity. When crafting content, ensure consistency in messaging, visual elements, and overall brand representation across different channels. Make sure to align your content with the established brand aesthetics to reinforce a unified and compelling brand identity as a cohesive brand image enhances recognition, trust, and loyalty.

Branding in AI: Steps to Ensure Seamless Integration

Generating branded content with the help of AI involves a strategic approach to ensure alignment with your brand identity. Here's a step-by-step guide:

1. **Define Your Brand Identity**

Clearly articulate your brand values, voice, and personality. Identify the key elements that define your brand, such as colours, tone, and messaging. This foundational step lays the groundwork for generating content that resonates with your brand identity.

2. **Create Brand Guidelines**

Develop comprehensive brand guidelines that outline the dos and don'ts of your brand's visual and verbal communication. Include details about logo usage, colour schemes, writing style, and any specific brand elements. These guidelines serve as a reference for maintaining consistency.

3. **Train the AI Model**

Provide the AI model with training data that reflects your brand's voice and historical content. This could include existing marketing materials, website content, and successful campaigns. By exposing the AI to your brand's style, it learns to generate content that aligns with your established identity.

Let's dive deeper into the process of training an AI model for creating branded content with an example.

Imagine you are a company known for your eco-friendly and sustainable products. Your brand identity revolves around nature, environmental consciousness, and innovation. To effectively train the AI model, follow these steps:

i. **Collect Relevant Data**

Gather marketing collateral, blog posts, social media content, and any other materials that showcase your brand's commitment to sustainability. Include content that has resonated well with your audience and has been successful in conveying your values.

ii. Identify Key Themes

Analyse the collected data to identify recurring themes, key messaging, and the specific language used to communicate your brand's eco-friendly initiatives. Pinpoint the phrases, tones, and sentiments that define your unique brand voice.

iii. Create a Training Corpus

Construct a training corpus that encapsulates these identified elements. This corpus should be a curated selection of sentences, paragraphs, and headlines that exemplify your brand's style. It serves as the primary source for teaching the AI model about your brand identity.

iv. Establish Guidelines

Develop explicit guidelines for the AI model based on your findings. Specify the preferred vocabulary, tone, and messaging style. If your brand is known for being approachable and friendly, ensure that these traits are emphasised in the guidelines.

v. Training Sessions

Conduct multiple training sessions where the AI model processes and learns from the training corpus. The model adapts to the language patterns, sentiment, and nuances inherent in your brand's communication style.

4. Fine-Tuning with Feedback

As the AI generates content, gather feedback from human reviewers who understand your brand well. Use this feedback to fine-tune the model, correcting any deviations and reinforcing the elements that align with your brand identity.

For instance, if your brand often uses phrases like 'Harmony with Nature' or 'Innovating for a Greener Tomorrow,' these become crucial elements in your training data. The AI model learns to incorporate these phrases organically when generating new content.

This strategic approach ensures that the AI becomes adept at reflecting your brand identity, ultimately contributing to the creation of branded content that resonates with your audience.

5. Craft Detailed Prompts

When generating content using AI, craft detailed prompts that incorporate your brand guidelines. Specify the desired tone, language, and style. The more precise your instructions, the better the AI can produce content that reflects your brand accurately. The following examples illustrate how you can enhance prompt generation.

Consider a scenario where you are a technology company aiming to generate content about the benefits of cloud computing. A generic prompt might look like this

> 'Generate content describing the advantages and applications of cloud computing in various industries.'

While this prompt can yield information about cloud computing, it lacks specificity about your brand's unique style and messaging. To elevate this prompt, we will need to incorporate specific branding instructions for a technology company committed to innovation and user-centric solutions.

> 'Craft a compelling piece outlining the transformative impact of cloud computing across industries, emphasising our brand's commitment to cutting-edge innovation and user-friendly solutions. Incorporate phrases like "Revolutionising Business Dynamics" and "Empowering Users with Seamless Connectivity." Ensure the tone is authoritative yet approachable, aligning with our brand's identity. Highlight real-world success stories and use terminology that reflects our dedication to simplifying complex technological concepts for our audience.'

In this detailed prompt, the brand's unique identity is infused into the instructions. Specific phrases, the preferred tone, and key messaging elements are provided, ensuring that the AI-generated content aligns precisely with the brand's ethos. This approach significantly enhances the likelihood of producing content that resonates with the audience and mirrors the brand's distinctive voice and values.

6. Review and Edit Outputs

Even though AI can assist in content creation, it is essential to review and edit the generated outputs. Ensure that the content aligns with your brand identity and adheres to the guidelines. Make necessary adjustments to maintain consistency.

7. **Human Oversight**

While AI can be a powerful tool, human oversight is crucial. Skilled professionals should have the final say in approving and fine-tuning the content. This ensures that the human touch, essential for brand authenticity, is preserved.

Key Takeaways

1. When crafting content, aim to evoke feelings and connect with your audience's aspirations to make your brand more relatable.
2. For your content, make sure to keep messaging and visuals uniform across all channels to strengthen brand recognition and trust.
3. To get AI-generated content spot-on, train your model with detailed brand guidelines and refine it based on feedback. This ensures the content reflects your brand's unique voice and keeps it aligned with your identity.

Checklist for Editing Generative AI Content

No.	Rubrics	Perfect	Partial	Negative
1	Spelling and Grammar	[ ]	[ ]	[ ]
2	Bias and Sensitivity	[ ]	[ ]	[ ]
3	Factuality	[ ]	[ ]	[ ]
4	Credibility & Sources	[ ]	[ ]	[ ]
5	Thorough Analysis	[ ]	[ ]	[ ]
6	Content Expansion	[ ]	[ ]	[ ]
7	Completeness	[ ]	[ ]	[ ]
8	Tone Appropriateness	[ ]	[ ]	[ ]
9	Conciseness	[ ]	[ ]	[ ]
10	Lexical Resources	[ ]	[ ]	[ ]
11	Coherence & Cohesion	[ ]	[ ]	[ ]

No.	Rubrics	Perfect	Partial	Negative
12	Creativity & Complexity	[ ]	[ ]	[ ]
13	Depth	[ ]	[ ]	[ ]
14	Formatting and Style	[ ]	[ ]	[ ]
15	Readability	[ ]	[ ]	[ ]
16	Branded Content	[ ]	[ ]	[ ]

Acknowledgements

LIFE BECOMES BEAUTIFUL WHEN YOU ARE SURROUNDED by the right people—those who have a way of softening the toughest moments. Once those moments pass, these same people will remind you of those difficult times in the most hilarious ways, making you laugh and feel as though the pain belonged to another lifetime. That's how you progress, and that's how you achieve success. One such person who has always stood by me, turning my pain and shortcomings into shine and giggles, is my husband. I thank Dr Dhaval Shah for being the partner with whom I have risen, fallen, and risen again.

When the days of my life became cloudy and I wanted to sulk, my two little ones, Kashish and Yuvraj, never let me. Their mere existence, with their questions and looks, is enough to make me smile. I thank them for being such wonderful children, always finding innovative ways to make me laugh and get frustrated at the same time. They are the reason I have goals, and they are the reason I believe life is so much more beautiful.

I extend my heartfelt gratitude to my mother, father, and sister, whose support in every aspect of life has been invaluable. To my extended family—cousins, nieces, nephews, uncles, and aunts—your belief in my abilities has been a pillar of strength.

A special thanks to Professor Nikhil Kant and Professor Siddharth Deshmukh for imparting deep insights into content marketing with practical knowledge that was both easy to learn and apply. Their teachings have been pivotal in writing this book.

I am deeply grateful to Hay House for taking on this project. I am confident they will help it achieve the highest level of success. Aditya Jarial's dedication to refining the content, ensuring it remains both engaging and accessible, has been instrumental in shaping *AI to A+* into the invaluable resource it is today. His meticulous attention to detail and commitment to maintaining the book's friendly tone have elevated it to new heights.

I would also like to extend my gratitude to Sunil Sihag, who expertly managed the pre-launch PR and played a crucial role in helping me reach my aspirations.

Lastly, a heartfelt thanks to Raghav Khattar for designing the book cover. Its vibrant green and yellow design is not only visually striking but also perfectly captures the modern and dynamic essence of the book. I am confident that the cover will attract readers and make a lasting impression.

Thank you all for being an integral part of this journey and for making every step of the way truly rewarding.

References

1. https://aicontentfy.com/en/blog/benefits-of-branded-content-in-marketing-strategy#:~:text=Branded%20content%20provides%20better%20storytelling,brand%20on%20an%20emotional%20level.
2. https://www.parse.ly/resource/content-matters-ai-trends-2023-report/
3. https://www.semrush.com/blog/branded-content/#
4. https://grin.co/blog/what-is-branded-content/
5. *Personal Branding for Dummies* by Susan Chritton
6. *Sticky Branding* by Jeremy Miller
7. *Branding: In Five and a Half Steps* by Michael Johnson

About the Author

Shanu Shah is a distinguished professional with expertise in literature, content planning and marketing, and leadership. As a celebrated author of several acclaimed titles, Shanu has been honoured with multiple awards, including the prestigious Most Influential Woman award for her literary achievements. With six years of experience in content planning, she has refined her creativity and strategic acumen to drive successful campaigns and build a robust online presence for businesses. Through her Substack (@ishanushah), Shanu continues to share valuable insights, empowering authors and content writers to reach their goals. Outside her professional endeavours, she enjoys playing table tennis, exploring new places with her family, and diving into thrilling novels.

For more from the author or to get in touch, you can follow Shanu Shah on LinkedIn, Substack, and Instagram (@ishanushah).